THE WRETCHES
OF
POVERTYVILLE

NASCHER

Wm Mutton

please return

THE HEAVEN AND HELL OF THE UNDERWORLD.

The Wretches of Povertyville

A Sociological Study of the Bowery

BY

I. L. NASCHER, M. D.

Sketches and Illustrations by George Toner

JOS. J. LANZIT, Publisher,
CHICAGO
1909

COPYRIGHTED 1904-1909
BY
I. L. NASCHER.

INTRODUCTION.

I watched some chips as they floated down the stream. Here and there one, swerved from the course by a straw, or a zephyr perhaps, approached an eddy, touched its edge and went circling round its whirls.

Now approaching, now receding from the channel, each turn brought it nearer the center; with each movement the fatal attraction toward the vortex became stronger, faster and faster it sped until it reached the vortex, then gave one last spin, one plunge, and disappeared.

I watched the lives of men as they floated down the stream of life.

A note, a sigh, a glass of wine or a woman's smile would swerve one from the straight and narrow channel. Slowly, unconsciously perhaps, he would be drawn toward the whirlpool which has perdition in its vortex. He reaches the outer whirl, scarcely realizing that he is off the course and going further and further away from the straight line.

He travels around the outer circle and is back again, but now there is a barrier between him and the true channel, an invisible barrier, a line in width, a wall in strength.

He is in a pleasant whirl with many companions, all rushing toward the same goal, all unconscious or unconcerned about the dark abyss at its end.

Spinning around faster and faster, he scorns the plodders in the narrow channel without, while the barrier between him and them becomes wider and stronger. He reaches the vortex, sees death therein and with a life's remorse compressed into a moment's pang, he is drawn below forever.

The stream of life which flows through Povertyville is not a gentle stream flowing between mossy banks, past pleasant scenes. It is a turbulent river, with rocky bottom and muddy banks, with few pleasant places along its course. In its channel are snags whereon the traveler suddenly ends his career; eddies and whirlpools which, once entered, drag the victim to destruction.

While many enter the whirlpool, ignorant of what its vortex holds, and others enter to enjoy its giddy whirl, careless of the abyss at its end, many seek the vortex to find oblivion. It does not disappoint them.

CONTENTS.

PART I

POVERTYVILLE.

		PAGE
Chapter	I.........The Underworld of Povertyville...	7
"	II.........The Backbone of Povertyville......	10
"	III.........The Evolution of the Bowery.....	34
"	IV.........Dives and Dens....................	43
"	V.........Homes and Haunts................	70

PART II

THE WRETCHES.

Chapter	I.........Pariahs	98
"	II.........Their Tempters and Parasites.....	112
"	III.........Factors Developing Wretches......	128
"	IV.........Some Curious Characters..........	146
"	V.........Slaves of the Pipe.................	168
"	VI.........Lives of the Wretches.............	184
"	VII.........Craft as a Science................	198
"	VIII.........Side Lights	225
"	IX.........The Final Accounting............	237

PART III

THE PROBLEM.

Chapter	I.........Philanthropy vs. Hypocrisy.......	248
"	II.........Impractical Ideals	259
"	III.........Practical Measures	272

PART I

POVERTYVILLE

POVERTYVILLE

CHAPTER I

THE UNDERWORLD OF POVERTYVILLE.

'TIS a wretched world, this underworld of Povertyville, where poverty begets vice, and vice begets crime, where virtue has its price, and conscience is stilled, then forgotten.

'Tis a dreary world, this world of sin, where every man has a companion and no man has a friend, where the past leaves no comfort, and the future brings no hope, where the gentle rays of salvation are shut out while the pall of perdition is ever present enfolding its tenants, itself invisible in the gloom.

'Tis a curious world, this world of crime, where humanity appears under strange lenses which here throw a halo and there cast a shadow, now presenting an exaggerated picture and again a diminutive outline, bringing some dull, prosaic life into high relief or dulling the sharp edges of a strong character until it is merged in the sombre background. A world where innocence is crime and virtue is weakness, where craft outweighs reason and brawn outweighs both, where happiness is found in another's grief and honor is sought in infamy.

'Tis a morbid world, this underworld of Povertyville, where Nemesis is ever present and ever threatening, though with broken bridle and open yoke, with the baton in place of the sword and the slow wheels of law replacing her chariot and wings. The fear of her vengeance is a blight upon it and lasts to the grave, but not beyond, for there is no hereafter in this underworld: it holds its heaven and its hell.

It holds a heaven where the sirens' songs are forever echoing, drowning the shrieks of their victims; where the bacchanalia ends with the last breath, ne'er marred by thought of cost, nor stopped by fear of a punitive hereafter.

And a hell such as Dante could never conceive of, a hell without a river Lethe to bestow hell's only blessing, forgetfulness. It is not in the fear of Satan and everlasting fires nor in the pains which afflict the body and harry the soul, that its tenants find the torments of the damned, but in memory, the memory of childhood, of mother, perhaps of wife and children, the memory of happier days before they entered the gates of the world wherein they dwell—that is their hell.

'Tis then they hear the still, soft voice within calling in agony to Him for salvation, but——

"Another drink, boys; take partners for the next dance."

Such is the underworld of Povertyville.

In the following description of the Bowery and its purlieu special stress has been laid upon the vicious phases of life found there. No attempt has been made to describe the homes and home life of the self-respecting poor families of the East Side. While vast improvements have been made in the social conditions in that district since Riis gave us his wonderful pen pictures of "How the other half lives" nearly twenty years ago, there is still the same poverty, and many of the problems that he pointed out are still problems. If not the greatest, certainly one of the most difficult problems of the East Side is the handling of the "wretches." The specific purpose of this work is to present these as they appear to the investigator.

CHAPTER II

THE BACKBONE OF POVERTYVILLE.

THE Bowery is the backbone of Povertyville.
Far back in Governor Stuyvesant's time a wooden bridge crossed a brook which flowed from the Kalck Water or Collect Pond, as it was afterwards called, to the East River. Dutch gallants crossing this bridge with their sweethearts exacted a toll in the shape of a kiss while crossing, and, if history records correctly, their rambles invariably led them to the farther side. This bridge, which stood at what is now the junction of Baxter Street and Park Row, was the beginning of a lane which led to the Governor's "Bouwerie," or farm, the Bouwerie Pathye of the Dutch, the Bowery Road of the English, the famous Bowery of New York to-day.

The Bowery had a pleasant beginning, and for two hundred and fifty years it has been a street of pleasure.

Yet it was not pleasure unalloyed, for while no other street can show in the same length such variety or such number of places given to man's entertainment and pleasures, no other street hides so much sorrow and shame, such poverty and depravity, such sights to arouse pity and sights to excite horror as this same Bowery.

POVERTYVILLE

Here Ike and Mike mix jargon and brogue over the bar of a German saloon; Francois and his ancient enemy, Fritz, under the firm name of Frank and Fred, sell old clothes, and the son of sunny Italy, with his partner, a cueless convert from China or a descendant of a Guinea slave, runs a pool room or a policy shop.

Here poverty lurks behind lace curtains and wealth hides behind muslin shades; here smiling faces conceal broken hearts and merry jests drown mournful sighs; here rich and poor, the educated and the illiterate, the man in the dress suit, and the man in rags, find a common level.

The Bowery is a street of contradictions. Open to the world, yet it is full of the mysterious. As well known abroad as the Whitechapel of London, and at home as Wall Street, as full of life at midnight as at midday, few of the thousands who traverse it by day know the midnight Bowery; fewer still have been behind the scenes of the stage upon which its wretches appear. Even the midnight wanderers, to whom the Bowery is home, know little, care less, about their neighbors or companions. To them the street outside of their own sphere is a terra incognito.

The Bowery has not its counterpart in the world. A cosmopolis in itself, it forms the boundary of half a dozen foreign colonies. Near its beginning there is an Irish colony, and near by is the only Greek colony in the city. North of the Greeks and stretching eastward to the river are Jews of five nationalities. There are Russian, Polish, Roumanian, Galician, and German Jews, each nationality having its own center, but with overlapping borders. North of these, but mingling with them at about Houston street, are the Hungarians, and beyond them is a remnant of Little Germany, which once completely filled the east side north of Houston street.

On the west side of the Bowery there is the famous Chinatown near the lower end, with Little Italy beyond and to the northward of the Mongolian quarter.

Near the upper end of the street there are a few of the American families who, half a century ago, made this the fashionable part of the city.

While each of these nationalities has added its quota to the mass who form the wretches of Povertyville, it is not until they have become Americanized, have adapted themselves to the environment of the district and adopted its ways and vices, that they become full-fledged wretches.

In its business aspect, the Bowery is contradictory. It has seven banks, including the richest savings bank in the country, and near them are three times as many pawnshops. Uncle Simpson's pawnshop (there are five bearing this name) is as well known as the Bowery Savings Bank; yet while the population in the vicinity of the Bowery is decreasing, the number of banks and pawnshops increases.

In its amusements the street once catered to the fashionable and refined, just as that part of Broadway from 28th to 48th streets does today. Now the language of the country is heard in but two of its nine theaters, and there it is not the language of the drawing room, but the patter of the coarse burlesque and low vaudeville stage. Of the others, one is a Chinese theater and six are Jewish.

The Italians had a theater on the Bowery in 1902, but neither drama nor vaudeville seemed to appeal to those for whom it was intended, and it soon closed its doors.

The Chinese Opera House in Doyers Street, near the Bowery, is the queerest theater in New York.

Externally the building resembles the rear of an old-fashioned tenement house, having, however, a row of windows always closed by iron shutters on the ground floor. The upper part is the rear of a Chatham Square lodging house. The entrance is like the ordinary tenement entrance, but just inside the door a space is partitioned off for the box office. The theater is a long hall a few feet below the street level, with a small stage in one corner. There are no flies, wings, curtains or scenery. Incidental property such as a table, chair, etc., is brought in when required in any part of the play and removed when it has served its purpose. The auditorium is filled with benches and as there is little pitch to the floor, late comers sit on the backs of the rear benches. Near the entrance and opposite the stage is the white visitors' private box, an enclosed platform holding a dozen chairs. The orchestra consists of three pieces—a gong, a drum, and either a "Njee Yen," or two-stringed fiddle, or a "Kin" or five-stringed instrument. The musicians sit on the stage near the door through which the performers appear. There are rarely more than three actors at one time on the stage, and the performance appears to be a succession of monologues, interspersed with short dialogues, pounding on the gong or drum and squeaking of the Njee Yen. Males take female parts, speaking in a shrill, piping voice. There are no programs, the stolid Chinamen never applaud, and the stranger can form no conception of the character of the play. Without the music one would as readily imagine it to be a lodge initiation, a prayer meeting or a political discussion as a theatrical performance. The other theaters are like theaters elsewhere.

The Thalia Theater, the Old Bowery of our youthful days, typifies the changes which have gone on in its neighborhood during the last three-quarters of a century.

The New York Theater, opened on this site in 1826, was in its day the finest theater in America. It was called Bowery Theater in 1827 and for forty years thereafter it was the home of good drama and good English, the English of Edwin Forrest, the two Wallacks, Rice, Quinn, Hamlin, and Charlotte Cushman. Then came the "blood and thunder" plays, four or five pieces every night, a villain killed in every act and the heroine saved in every scene. The changes in the character of the plays were reflections of the changes in the character and tastes of the Bowery audiences. In 1879 it became a German theater and received its present name. It is now a Jewish theater, the performances being given in the colloquial German of the Russian Jew. (This jargon is a philological curiosity; being a German dialect, containing many Russian, Polish and Hebrew words, and used by the Jews in Roumania, Hungary, southern and western Russia, is generally spoken among the Jews in the "Ghettos" of Europe).

The plays themselves are either dramas founded upon Jewish historical incidents or adaptations from popular German or English plays, and are performed by stock companies.

Opposite the Thalia Theater is Windsor Theater, another Jewish playhouse formerly giving performances in English. It stands on the site of Stadt Theater, the most famous German theater in America from 1859 to 1879.

The People's Theater, erected in 1883 to furnish refined drama, has gone jargonward. In the early sixties Pastor's Opera House was on this site. In the seventies it was occupied by the German Volks Garten, and this was followed by the present theater. As a home of refined drama it was a dismal failure, but it became successful when lurid melodramas were placed upon its boards. Now as a Jewish theater it is more successful than ever.

The little old National Theater, between Grand and Hester streets, now the Manhattan Music Hall, has been converted into a Jewish vaudeville house. Jewish vaudeville is an innovation of doubtful success, two concert halls, the Casino Music Hall, near Stanton Street, and the Grand Street Music Hall on Grand Street near the Bowery, having failed soon after introducing this feature. There are, however, several Jewish music halls in the district which seem to be successful. The finest theater on the East Side is the new Grand Theater on Grand Street, one block east of the Bowery. This is a Jewish playhouse which, in its appointments, character of plays and work, compares favorably with Broadway theaters. The principal actor of the Stock Company, Jacob Adler, created quite a stir in theatrical circles in 1902 when he appeared with an English-speaking company at the American Theater. The play, the Merchant of Venice, was given in English, except the part of Shylock rendered by Mr. Adler in jargon. (This theater is giving English melodrama at present.)

In the two English-speaking houses, the London Theater and Miner's Theater, the performances given are alike—coarse burlesques, low vaudeville, sometimes boxing and wrestling. While individual numbers may be clean and equal to the work seen in the best vaudeville houses in the city, the frequenters of these theaters want what they call a "hot show," one coming as close to the line of indecency as the law will allow. The delicate suggestiveness of the modern society play would be lost upon the audiences found in either of these two houses. In the after piece, as the closing act of the burlesque show is called, the actions are often coarsely suggestive, the talk vile. Yet these two theaters are the only ones catering to the English-speaking East Sider, and they are well patronized.

There are two types of concert or music hall on the Bowery.

The permanent type, of which the Atlantic Garden is the only one remaining, is run in conformity with the law, and the ephemeral type, which runs in violation of the law and depends upon the temper of the police and the political status of the manager or backer for its existence—not one of these is now found in the district.

The Atlantic Garden is the oldest place of amusement in the city with the exception of the Thalia Theater, which it adjoins. (The Academy of Music was first opened in 1854, four years before the Atlantic Garden, but the present Academy of Music was erected in 1866.) The performances given here are vaudeville of no high order of merit, but clean and unobjectionable. It is one of the few music halls in the city to which a man can take his wife and daughter without being compelled to listen to vulgar jokes and questionable songs. It is not popular with those who look for depravity. The Atlantic Garden was originally an open-air garden at the back of the New York Hotel. About 1860 the hotel feature was given up, and later the garden part was roofed over, a stage put up and vaudeville numbers introduced.

In the seventies it was popular with the Germans and then, as now, it was distinguished from similar places in the vicinity by its clean performances.

There is a type of music hall on the Bowery which keeps within the letter of the law but approaches the line of indecency so closely that no man would take his family into it. This type, of which there are several in the district, will be described in the chapter on "Dives and Dens."

Among the latest additions to the Bowery amusements is the "Penny Arcade." This owes its origin to the introduction of the slot machine. A store is filled with such machines, including phonographs, moving pictures, weighing machines, X-ray machines, lung testers, automatic banjos and pianos, faradic batteries, moving models of fire engines, locomotives and steamships, cameras, punching bags, etc. Admission is free, the only charge being a cent in the slot of any machine the visitor wishes to use. These places are fruitful fields for the pickpocket. There are also several moving picture shows on the street.

Among the Bowery amusements may be included the Museums. The reputable museums of twenty years ago are gone and in their stead exhibitions professing to be museums are opened and run for a few weeks, or until complaint is made to the police.

In one such place the placards announced that the female form was there on exhibition in all its loveliness. The visitor paid five cents and was admitted to a room containing a few panoramic views of towns and photographs of stage beauties. When several visitors were collected in this room a guide entered and informed them that upon a further payment of ten cents they would be admitted to the sanctum sanctorum, where this beautiful female form could be seen through a slit in the curtain. The curious visitor saw through this slit a dressmaker's dummy figure with flesh-colored tights filled with hay.

One museum had placards announcing in the most extravagant terms that it contained the eighth wonder of the world; admission ten cents. This wonder was a stuffed four-legged chicken. The whole hall was covered with theatrical posters and in one corner was a fortune teller's tent.

Another museum opened a short time ago has a few wax figures in the window. Inside there are a few wax figures hardly worth the price of admission. A visitor is accompanied by an attendant who induces him to touch the handles of an electric battery and then compels him to pay for electrical treatment.

An anatomical museum has been on the Bowery for a number of years. This is a bare remnant of a once famous Broadway museum of the same name and contains a number of anatomical specimens, wax casts, artificial monstrosities and medical plates. The exhibition itself is poor and would hardly pay, but credulous visitors are sometimes inveigled into the doctor's office, the phrenologist's room or the palmist's corner and there cajoled or frightened into paying a dollar or two for services rendered.

In every museum on the Bowery some scheme is worked whereby the visitor is compelled to pay something for "services rendered."

More noticeable than its places of amusement are its saloons occupying one-sixth of the entire number of stores on the two streets (Park Row and the Bowery). The saloons were a feature of the Bowery ever since Wolfert Webber opened his tavern near the Kissing Bridge, and that was long before the English planted their flag over New Amsterdam. Then came a century or more of taverns, the Bull's Head, the most famous of all, standing for seventy years on the site of Thalia Theater. At the beginning of the last century the gardens appeared on the thoroughfare.

The Vauxhall Garden was the first to be opened; the Atlantic Garden is the only one remaining today. About 1840 the ale houses made their appearance, and of this type there is one left. McSorley's Old House at Home in 7th Street, near the Bowery, is an inconspicuous place rarely visited by strangers. It has still the massive tables and chairs, with one long table in the back room, a bare-looking bar with a row of pewter mugs hanging on the wall behind; the sanded floor, dingy ceiling, the walls covered with lithographs and engravings of a former generation. Its old ale, the clay pipes and tobacco, furnished free to its patrons, and the air of "old times" which surrounds it make it attractive to a lot of old boys, young boys when it was opened near its present site fifty years ago.

It is impossible to classify the Bowery saloons of today. There is one which makes a specialty of German wines, the quality and price of which attract connoisseurs and deter the ordinary Bowery throng. It is a favorite resort for the German merchants of the neighborhood and needs no tinsel, music or advertising to retain a good class of patrons.

Adjoining it is a "Morgue," so called in the parlance of the street because the stuff dispensed there brings the consumer in time to its more gruesome namesake. It attracts by the size of its glasses; the quality would drive away the least fastidious. On a side street nearby is a "barrel house" where casks take the place of bottles behind the bar. When a customer asks for his favorite brand, a small tumbler is filled to the brim and handed to him after he has produced the necessary five cents. The contents disappear at a gulp. When beer is ordered in these places the customer orders a "tub" and receives a glass holding nearly a pint.

Another saloon of the same kind announces the largest drink on the Bowery for a nickel. It is run by a former actor, and many who once appeared behind the footlights now hang about its bar.

Steve Brodie's Saloon near Grand Street defies classification. Its squalid exterior would never tempt the thirsty stranger, but no slumming guide will pass the place without entering, unless ladies are in the party. Its interior is as forbidding as the outside, but the walls are covered with programs, pictures, gloves and relics, the delight of the admirer of fistiana and curiosities, while on the bar and scattered about are objects and signs indicative of the broad and coarse humor of the Bowery. It has two classes of patrons—slumming parties and wretches. The rear room is an ordinary dive. The place changed hands in the summer of 1908, and some of the vicious features were removed.

One saloon, an ordinary looking place hardly worth a second glance, is the most attractive place on the street to the denizens of Povertyville, especially of the underworld. It is the rendezvous of the lieutenants of Povertyville's autocrat, the Hon. Timothy D. Sullivan. "Big Tim," as they call him, is rarely found here, but when his advice is sought or a politician's services are required, the preliminaries are arranged at its bar or in its side room.

A small place not far from Brodie's was at one time a model of neatness and became famous through the skill of the proprietor in mixing drinks. He afterward published a standard barkeepers' manual. The place was later run by a reformed burglar and was frequented by many of his former prison associates. It is now an ordinary liquor store.

There is an old corner saloon which was thirty years ago a famous resort for horsemen. It is now patronized by gamblers and small sports.

Almost every saloon on the Bowery has its particular class of patrons. Saloons run by sports or politicians attract these classes. A corner saloon on the Bowery, not far from police headquarters, is a rendezvous for police officials. Some saloons are merely adjuncts to dives. These will be considered in the chapter on Dives and Dens.

The stale beer dives which sold stale beer collected from the nearly empty beer kegs, for a cent or two cents a glass, have gone out of existence, thanks to the introduction of the beer pump, by which saloonkeepers can drain the keg dry.

No church edifice was ever erected on the Bowery, although there are thirty representing half as many denominations within a block or two of it. The only sectarian institutions on the street are two missions, the headquarters of the Volunteers of America, a branch of the Salvation Army and a branch of the Young Men's Christian Association. It is remarkable that this thoroughfare, one of the oldest in the city, where evangelical work would probably do more good than anywhere else, has been thus neglected.

As a residence street the Bowery shows a peculiar condition. It was once lined with residences throughout its length. Now there are few families living on the street, and most of these are the families of the small Bowery storekeepers. Yet more than twenty-five thousand persons spend their nights in its one hundred or more lodging houses and hotels, or sleep as soundly on casks and chairs in the rear of its saloons. The number is increased shortly before election day, while hundreds of the winter residents leave the city in the spring when tramping is good.

To supply this floating population there are about seventy-five restaurants, but not one grocery store or butcher shop can be found from Brooklyn Bridge to Cooper Union.

No other street in the city can show such extremes in its trading places nor in the variety of goods sold.

For the sale of men's apparel there are one hundred and fifteen stores; for the sale of woman's wear there is not one. Among its clothing stores there are some which in quality and price equal the best on Broadway; some sell old clothes as new, some sell only second-hand clothing, and even new clothing is sold as second hand on the Bowery. Neither the size of the store nor the window display is a safe criterion by which to judge the character of the place.

Just beyond the official end of the Bowery there is a large establishment which in the quality and prices of its wares rivals the fashionable Broadway clothing stores, and its name is a guarantee of excellence. Not far away is another establishment which makes the most pretentious display on the street. This is another of the few reliable Bowery clothing stores; its prices are somewhat higher than the prices current on the Bowery for similar goods, though lower than Broadway prices. Near by is a place where old and new clothing are sold. The prospective purchaser here is never certain that he is getting what he wants. Even if he calls for a second-hand suit he may get a cheap new suit, apparently worn, bearing the name of a fashionable tailor.

Further down the street are several stores making considerable window display, with alluring prices, but rarely will a purchaser get the clothing at the prices marked unless they are misfits, that is, suits made to order and not fitting the customers who ordered them.

In many stores where clothes are made to order, bargaining is the rule. The experienced purchaser first looks at the goods, asks the price, then asks to see the lining, buttons, etc., and having made his selection he begins to "beat down" on the price. He will offer half, the dealer will accept three-fourths and they compromise on two-thirds of the price originally asked. Having given a deposit he demands a sample of the goods, lining and buttons, otherwise he may not get the material selected. The fit and workmanship will generally be found satisfactory.

In the small clothing stores, especially those in which

the interior is dark, the best goods are poor and the cheapest are dear at any price. Bargaining is the invariable rule in stores selling second-hand goods. Some of these stores are in basements or hallways, and the entire stock is near the door. They have queer methods by which they replenish their stock. Some come from the "fences" or dealers in stolen goods. Some come from the dealers whose familiar cry "any cast clothes" is heard in all parts of the city. When a death has occurred in a family a dealer visits the house of mourning the day following the funeral and either begs for the clothing of the deceased or offers to buy them. In some parts of the city the dealer goes around in a wagon and offers tinware and crockery for old clothes, shoes, hats, etc. When the stock is low he will buy a lot of auction trash, either goods spoilt in the making or goods put together in the cheapest manner possible, to be sold at auction; such goods are then slightly wrinkled, the name band of some well-known clothier is attached, and they are sold as second-hand. Unless the would-be purchaser knows the tricks and ways of second-hand clothing dealers he will be deceived. This applies to almost all stores where both new and second-hand goods are sold.

The extremes found in clothing stores in the Bowery district are also found in its hat and shoe stores. Some Bowery hatters are as well and favorably known as hatters in fashionable districts, their prices are lower than Broadway prices for the same quality and they do not deceive customers. At the other extreme are hatters who do not occupy stores but hire a room on an upper floor. One of these sells only new hats, but they are not in the prevailing style and no one knows what becomes of the old hats brought there every night by dealers in second-hand clothing.

A few places sell only old hats refurbished. They buy them for a few cents apiece, clean and reblock them, put in a new sweat band and lining and sell them for from 20 to 60 cents. In the shoe stores there is little chance for deception, but bargaining will generally avail. In some, where standard brands are sold, the salesman receives a commission on his sales and he will always share his commission with a purchaser.

There are several dealers in second-hand shoes on the Bowery and in the "Bay," as the vicinity of Baxter Street and Park Row is called. They buy the shoes from rag dealers and dealers in second-hand clothing, patch them up, put on heels and soles and polish them. These bring from 50 to 75 cents a pair.

Among the fifty jewelry stores between Brooklyn Bridge and Cooper Union there are a few which are honestly conducted, where gold is sold as gold and brass as brass. Many are unreliable and in the pawnbroker's sales stores even experts are sometimes deceived. The window displays are fair criterions of the character of these establishments, as most of them display there whatever they have of value.

The largest jewelry store on the Bowery is just below Broome Street. This is one of the few stores where they do not permit bargaining and they charge prices according to the value of the article. These prices are high according to Bowery standards, though less than prices on Broadway.

A small place near Canal Street was opened by a German when that part of the city was frequented by wealthy Germans forty years ago. He still sticks to the old spot, although his former patrons have long since left the neighborhood. Another one of these old-timers is a short distance below. They conduct their business now as they did before the era of bargaining began on the Bowery, and are as reliable now as then. In most stores, however, bargaining is the rule and a purchaser who is not an adept at this method of doing business will pay more than the article purchased is worth.

In the pawnbrokers' sales store the purchaser of jewelry, unless he be an expert, is almost certain to be imposed upon. The dealers are shrewd judges of the quality and value of jewelry, and only in estimating the value of curios are they liable to be misled. The curio-hunter will pick up real bargains if he does not show too great concern about getting what he wants. If he offers to pay whatever the dealer asks the dealer at once assumes that his price was much too low and he will decline to sell it. If the purchaser will offer a quarter of the dealer's price he will probably get it at half. No one should ever buy an expensive article in a pawnbroker's sales store unless he knows the value of the article. It should be remembered that everything is second-hand and no manufacturer's or dealer's guarantee holds good on such articles.·

The source of the goods found in pawnbrokers' sales stores is as varied as in second-hand clothing stores. Some are purchased at pawnbrokers' sales, some at ordinary auction sales. The fence disposes of his property to the pawnbrokers' sales stores, after having changed it so as to be unrecognizable by the real owner. Most of the "fake" jewelry finds its way into these stores. Very little is purchased from strangers.

A comparatively new business is the trade in pawn tickets. Persons pawning articles which they cannot or do not wish to redeem, sell the ticket to a pawn ticket dealer. If the article is valuable and is pledged for a small amount, the dealer redeems it and pawns it again for the largest amount obtainable. When a ticket is placed on sale within a short time after it has been issued, the pledger has secured the largest amount possible on the article. When a ticket is offered shortly before its expiration, the pledger was probably unable to redeem the pledge and sold the ticket for anything he could get. If the article is worth redeeming the dealer redeems it, otherwise he risks a few cents in the purchase of the ticket, for which he will charge a dollar or two if he can dispose of it.

Sometimes a pledger requests the pawnbroker to issue the ticket for a larger amount than the pledger receives on the article pawned. The larger the amount loaned the more valuable the article is supposed to be and the more the ticket will bring. Of course this is only done when it is the intention of the pledger to dispose of the ticket. When one intends to purchase a ticket from the pawn ticket dealer, the purchaser goes to the pawnshop accompanied by the dealer's clerk, to see the goods he intends to purchase. The pownbroker charges 25 cents for showing the goods. The pawnshops on Park Row and the Bowery are generally reliable, that is, they do not issue "raised" pawn tickets nor do they drop tickets. Dropping tickets is an old trick. The pawnbroker buys a lot of cheap, plated jewelry and each piece is entered as a pledge, tickets ranging from one to five dollars being issued. A ticket is dropped wherever many people pass. The finder will either redeem what he believes to be an honest pledge or will pay 25 cents for the privilege of seeing the pawned article. If the finder does not think the article is worth redeeming he will try to sell the ticket, the purchaser again paying the fee for showing the goods. The first fee of 25 cents is probably more than the original cost of the article.

Besides these business places which any one can see when passing, there are several peculiar occupations conducted on the Bowery, legitimate in their way, yet secret. One of these is the manufacture of curiosities and monstrosities for museums. Mermaids, two-headed calves, four-legged chickens, etc., are made here to order. In another establishment relics are manufactured. They turn out ancient coins, old violins, old worm-eaten furniture, flint spear heads, "genuine" old masters' paintings, crosses and boxes made of wood taken from the Mount of Olives, armor with certificates to prove that it was worn by some famous knight, guns, swords, and bullets picked up on famous battle fields, in fact, everything which can be produced cheaply, can pass as a historical or curious relic and the authenticity of which cannot be disproved.

Within a few doors of the Bowery is a shop where crooked gambling utensils are made. They turn out marked cards, loaded and shaped ice, brace faro boxes and crooked roulette wheels.

In Elizabeth Street (one block west of the Bowery) there is a place where weapons for the criminal classes are made. Besides the revolver which they buy at the pawnbroker's sale store, the professional criminals occasionally use a black jack, loaded billy, brass knuckles, stiletto, etc.

The black jack is a leather bag about six inches long. The upper end is about an inch wide and filled with fine shot. The lower end is sewed around a piece of rope and forms an admirable handle. A thong at the lower end is intended to pass around the wrist. A blow on the head from the black jack will knock a man senseless without breaking his skull. The loaded billy is a small club with a piece of lead in a cavity in the lower end. The brass knuckles is a piece of iron or brass about four inches long and half an inch wide with four holes in it for the fingers. The under side is shaped to fit the hand when the hand is closed, and the upper side is left as a long bar or shaped like rings. A blow struck with it generally breaks the bone.

The ordinary Italian stiletto is a crude double-edged narrow blade about ten inches long, with a plain wooden handle. The sandbag requires no skill in its manufacture and is generally made by the criminal himself. A child's stocking, a salt bag or a bag made of any stout material is taken, the lower part is filled with sand tightly pressed in, and a string is tied around the part holding the sand. The upper part forms the handle. This acts like the black jack. A piece of lead pipe is sometimes used instead.

Another extraordinary occupation is that of slumming guide. Slumming parties usually get a police official to show them the sights. Those who do not know how to reach the officials either get a guide from a hotel or ask a barkeeper in a saloon on the Bowery to get some one to show them around. In the Chinatown district there are several saloons where such guides are found, and guides offer their services on the street. They show, in addition to the joss house, theater and restaurants, an opium joint, and if there are no ladies in the party, some of the vilest of the dives. Some of these guides show places which the police either do not know, dare not show or cannot obtain admission to. The guides who offer their services on the street are as reliable as the saloon guides, charge less and, while most are shabbily dressed and coarse, they are interesting characters and can make the trip taken under their guidance interesting.

Park Row, north of the bridge, and the Bowery contain 560 houses. Of these, 425 are occupied in whole or part by saloons, cigar stores, lodging houses, restaurants, places dealing in men's apparel and places which are patronized almost exclusively by men.

With the exception of the Jewish theaters, the Atlantic Garden and the dives, its places of amusement are intended for men alone. There are shops on the street which employ women and these are seen in the morning and evening hours going to and from their work. At other times the Bowery is pre-eminently the man's street in Povertyville.

CHAPTER III

EVOLUTION OF THE BOWERY.

THE history of the Bowery is as curious as the street itself. The history of the Bowery takes in what was originally known as the Bowery Road, which includes the present Park Row. It began as an Indian trail winding about the foot of the hills which extended along the length of Manhattan Island, skirting the marshes which bordered the island on the east. This is the only street in the city which follows an Indian trail throughout its length, the bend at Chatham Square still indicating where it swept around the foot of Werpoes, the Indian name of a hill the summit of which is now Park and Mott streets.

When the early Dutch settlers established their farms or "Bouweries" north of the hill, they followed this trail when going to and from the city, and as early as 1647 it was recognized as a highway. After Governor Stuyvesant pre-empted the land from Corlears Hook to about 30th Street, east of the road, for his Bouwerie and built his house near the present St. Mark's Church, he ordered the road widened to his house. This road, completed in 1651, was called the Bouwerie Patje, or Bouwerie Weg, now the Bowery. In 1689 the road was extended northward as a carriage road and ran to the Harlem Settlement and Kingsbridge. This extension, called Boston Road, Kingsbridge Road, Harlem Road, etc., is wiped out, except St. Nicholas Avenue and a part of upper Broadway.

The earliest road out of the city was the Breede Weg or Broadway, which followed its present line to City Hall Park, then along Park Row to about Baxter Street, where it ended at a brook which was here crossed by the Kissing bridge. North of this bridge was the Bouwerie Weg or Bowery, the only road leading out of the city until the early part of the last century. The earliest dwellers on the road were a number of manumitted slaves, who, in 1644, established their farms on the hill west of Chatham Square (Werpoes) and had their cattle pasture east of the road, covering part of the present square. After Governor Stuyvesant established his farm east of the Bowery, farms were taken up on the west side of the street.

About the middle of the 18th century the Bowery was a broad country road bordered by large estates. The Delancey farm extended from Chatham Square to about Houston Street. What is now Delancey Street, between Bowery and Chrystie Street, was originally the private lane to the Delancey mansion. The tract north of Houston Street was divided among the heirs of the Dutch Governor. Stuyvesant Street, which marks the limit of the Bowery, was the lane leading to the Governor's house and is the only street remaining of the original Bowery village except the main road itself.

West of the Bowery was the Bayard estate north of Canal Street, with the mansion at about Broadway and Broome Streets, Broome Street being on the line of the lane leading from the Bowery to the house. South of the Bayard estate was the Pell estate and smaller estates, the land being cut up into building lots. There was a cattle market south of Canal Street with the famous Bull's Head Tavern adjoining and a few dwellings south. In 1770 there were twelve licensed liquor vendors between the cattle market and the Commons (City Hall Park), and one in Bowery village about where 4th Avenue and 14th Street intersect. Long before the Revolution the lower end of the Bowery became what the street has been ever since, a street for pleasure-seekers. Within a couple of hundred feet of where the first kissing bridge stood there has been a pleasure garden or a theater from 1661 till 1861.

Near the upper end of the Bowery stood the Bowery tavern, famous in Colonial history as the meeting place of the first Colonial Congress in 1690, when the New England commissioners refused to enter the city on account of the prevailing yellow fever. At this tavern was celebrated annually, on St. John's day, the feast of St. John's, those whose given name was John participating. The tavern keeper, John Clapp, became locally famous, having introduced the first hackney coach for hire in 1696 and the first almanac the following year.

During the Revolution the Bowery, being the only road leading to the city, became one of the most frequented streets. A line of fortifications crossed the city from Fort Pitt, about where Pitt and Grand streets meet, to Richmond Hill Fort, at about Spring and Thompson streets. A circular fort at the present junction of Forsyth and Broome streets and another on Bayard Hill, near where Grand and Mott streets cross, commanded the Bowery Road and troops were encamped from these forts along both sides of the road to the Commons, now City Hall Park.

From Grand Street to the Commons, scores of drinking places and dance halls were opened for the accommodation of the troops, and at this early day the lower end of the Bowery Road, as it was then called, had acquired an unenviable reputation. The structures erected for the entertainment of the troops were of a temporary character and disappeared at the end of the war.

It was not until after the Revolution that the Bowery itself showed any signs of activity. The Delancey and the Pell estates were confiscated by the state government, sold and cut up into building lots.

This was the beginning of the Bowery as a residence street, although dwellings had already appeared at its lower and upper ends.

A few of these early buildings are still standing. A house on Pell Street, a few feet from the Bowery, is pointed out as the last home of the mythical Charlotte Temple, and a house near it on the Bowery has been occupied as a drug store since 1807.

The career of the Bowery as a street of pleasure resorts began in 1797, when the second Vauxhall Gardens were opened on the Bayard Farm after the original Vauxhall Gardens on Greenwich Street were closed. Five years later the garden was removed to Sperry's Botanical Garden, which extended from about 4th Street to Astor Place, west of Bowery to Broadway. The last part of this famous resort was closed in 1855. Among the famous resorts of this time were the Crown and Thistle coffee house at about 96 Bowery, the Pig and Whistle Inn at 131, and the Duck and Frying Pan Tavern on the east side of the Bowery just above North, now Houston, Street.

In the early thirties the Bowery was still a residence street, almost every house having a garden patch behind it and a hitching post in front. A number of houses of this period are still standing.

At the same time it had become more fully fixed as a street of pleasure. There were the American Theater (later Bowery Theater), the finest theater in the country, at its lower end, and the Vauxhall Gardens at the upper end of the street; the Gotham Garden was opened north of Houston Street, and taverns had made their appearance. On Park Row were Franklin Theater near Oliver

Street, Chatham Theater near Roosevelt Street, and Blanchard's Amphitheater, formerly Chatham Garden, near Pearl Street.

Before the Civil War the Bowery had become the most popular thoroughfare in New York. The staid old American families had left the neighborhood, that exaggerated type of American known as the "Bowery Boy" had appeared, and the German invasion had begun. The German Stadt Theater, the Deutcher Volks Garden and the Atlantic Garden had been opened, there was now a new Bowery Theater near Hester Street, as well as the old Bowery Theater near Canal Street, and a number of new garden resorts.

The character of the street and its frequenters had entirely changed in a quarter of a century. There were many small stores on the thoroughfare, but no imputation of doubt or distrust rested upon its merchants.

The broadest and brightest street in the city at that time, it attracted all who liked crowds and excitement and drove away the quiet-loving and refined families of the former generation. It had become a street with a reputation. With the close of the war there came another change. The boys in blue, flushed with victory and with the savings of years in their pockets, came to the Metropolis. The Bowery was the magnet, for there were now theaters, concert halls, gambling houses and dives, a blind police force and a worse than blind administration.

It was the beginning of the golden era of the Bowery's prosperity (for vice often prospers in spite of a punitive hereafter and a policeman's night stick).

A decade later the Bowery was a street of glittering vice, while the "Tenderloin" was still in its infancy.

There were the Sans Souci, the Louvre, the Moulin Rouge, the Jardin Mabille and a score of similar places, with colored glass lamps, flaming posters and red curtains, behind which black-eyed damsels tapped on windows to attract the attention of the uninitiated. The curious novice who entered one of these places generally paid the female vampires whatever of value he had about him and then came off cheaply.

And the peripatetic sisterhood was found all along the thoroughfare, paying their police protectors liberally for the privilege of occupying choice dark corners and even for walking along the street.

The Bowery had become disreputable.

Another decade and we find another change. It was still a street of pleasure, but vice was disappearing, most of the dives and foul resorts were gone and a foreign population had invaded the street. It was in a transition stage. Business houses were taking the place of its dives and concert halls, merchants were coming to the Bowery and it was fast losing its unsavory reputation, when a peculiar incident occurred to throw it back to the days of the early seventies. The song "The Bowery," where "they do such things and they say such things," appeared.

and its catchy air made it popular. Never did a popular song have a more pernicious effect. The notoriety of the Bowery was at once revived, business men would not establish themselves on the street, building operations ceased, real estate values dropped and the improvement in the street received a sudden check. Reputable merchants who had been in business on the Bowery for years were obliged to move away to escape the odium cast upon the street and reflected upon themselves.

Their place was taken by the disreputable class who had been stigmatized in the song, and in a short time the Bowery fully deserved all the notoriety which the song had forced upon it.

There was, however, a marked difference between the disreputable class of 1887 and that of 1877. The latter was the class now found in the Tenderloin, the places were bright, full of light and color, there was an air of prosperity about them, and as there was no elevated structure to darken the street, tinsel could be used effectively. Vice was made attractive to the novice and many of its votaries who later patronized the fashionable vicious resorts of the Tenderloin were found at that time on the Bowery. In 1887 the Bowery was dark, dull and gloomy, a foreign population had invaded it and its resorts were poor in appearance and attracted only a poor and unresponsive throng. The presence of the unsightly elevated structure was mainly responsible for the changed appearance of the Bowery.

Since then the foreign element has taken possession of the street and has monopolized its pleasures. The trade of the street, except its saloons, is mainly in the hands of Americanized Jews.

Today the Bowery is again in a transition stage, and what promises to be a permanent improvement in its character is now taking place. Its concert halls are going and almost gone, and with them the "Barker" and the "Bouncer," the one strong of voice to lure the wretches in, the other strong of arm to throw them out.

The colored lamps and curtains are gone, let us hope forever, and even the midnight wanderers who formerly stood at choice corners, waiting for victims, no longer ply their trade at their accustomed stands. True, they can still be found on the street, their painted cheeks, furtive glances and barely audible whispers as they hurry past a possible patron, revealing their vocation. But law and order have driven them from the street and into the rear rooms of the dives, where they are out of sight of all but those who seek them.

Business houses are now replacing many notorious resorts, magnificent buildings are in process of erection along the thoroughfare, vice, its haunts and votaries are carefully hidden from the public gaze, and the shady reputation of the Bowery is fast disappearing.

But to those who know the open sesame there are still its dives and dance halls, its gambling houses, its opium joints, its sporting houses and all that went to make up the Bowery of old.

INTERIOR OF A BOWERY DIVE AND DANCE HALL.

CHAPTER IV

DIVES AND DENS.

THERE is no sharp dividing line between the respectable saloon and the dive, between the clean music hall and the vicious concert hall, between the reputable bar-room and the disreputable dance hall. There is a wide difference between the extremes, but there are many grades between them.

There is the saloon to which women are not admitted, which has no family entrance or side room, and which offers no attraction or inducement to the vicious.

There is the saloon which has a private office reached from a side entrance, with a table and a couple of chairs. There is the saloon with a small back room having several tables, and reached through the side entrance, where men may take their female companions but women unaccompanied by men are not admitted. And thus the grade goes down to the low dive, with its small, bare-looking bar-room and its large rear room holding a score or more of tables, twice as many chairs, its piano and piano professor, its waiters, its bouncer, its satyrs, and its nymphs. The barroom is used only to supply the waiters and negatively to announce the presence of a rear room.

This room is reached through a side or "family" entrance, and here the women assemble after dark, drink, plan and make appointments with the men who seek them.

The professor thumps the piano, his foot upon the open pedal to increase the volume of sound so that it may be heard on the street, but neither melody nor harmony is expected. Occasionally one of the habitues or a waiter will sing a popular air, with piano accompaniment, but delicacy of touch, word or sentiment is not appreciated. The dive is not patronized by day, but as soon as darkness sets in the women arrive, generally in pairs, followed by their lovers. A few waiters are on hand, the headwaiter acting in the dual capacity of overseer and bouncer. The manager sits near the door where he can overlook the place, observe each newcomer and watch the waiters as they emerge from the barroom with drinks. The women in the dives are without exception disreputable, the men are their lovers, those seeking the favors of the mercenary sybarites, and sightseers.

The last are not popular, receive scant courtesy, and unless they order drinks frequently they are made to feel that their presence is undesirable.

If a visitor sits at a table at which a woman is seated he is expected to treat her. Formal introductions are unknown. "Say, Sis, what's yours?" combines the introduction, the invitation to drink and the opening of a conversation leading to business.

If the visitor is a stranger she will order sherry, for which he will pay 25 cents, but if he is a frequenter of such places he will deliberately order two beers and she will rarely refuse. The knowing ones order seltzer water or a shell of beer, the shell being a small, thin tumbler.

The "professor" is expected to play from dark to midnight, and loud enough to drown ordinary conversation, but he can never play so loud as to drown the waiter's "Give your orders, gents!" The sightseer is perfectly safe in the ordinary dive so long as he remains sober, sticks to seltzer water or beer, is provided with small change and does not lose his temper.

If he loses his temper he is liable to be thrown out; if he gives a large bill to the waiter, the latter may decamp or practice the flimflam game, a sleight-of-hand trick whereby he extracts a bill after having counted the change in the presence of the visitor. When a visitor is partly intoxicated one of the wretches will sit on his lap, throw one arm around his neck in a fond embrace, and while he is enjoying her caresses, her other hand is disengaging his watch and emptying his pockets.

The booty is passed to her lover who sits behind her. If the victim creates a disturbance when discovering his loss, the bouncer's services are brought into requisition.

The dives of a generation ago were bright, fairly well furnished, with some attempt at ornamentation. The Bowery dive of today is a bare, repellant place.

The most notorious in recent years was McGurk's Sporting House, commonly known as Suicide Hall. It received its gruesome pseudonym after several of its frequenters committed suicide there. The saloon part in front was bare of furniture except a bar and a back bar. It was rarely patronized. Behind the saloon, and separated from it by a partition, was a large room holding thirty tables, over a hundred chairs and a piano. The walls, where not bare, were hidden behind theatrical posters and lithographs. The owner's station was near one corner, from which he could overlook the place without being seen from the entrance, while the head-waiter and bouncer, an ex-pugilist, stood near the door. The entrance to the rear room was through a hall adjoining the saloon, the entrance from the saloon being used by the waiters. This place was crowded nightly, every woman from the street drifting in once or oftener in the course of the evening. The place was popular with soldiers and sailors, and its cards were found in sailors' resorts all over the world. Notwithstanding its notorious character it had a singular record. If a woman robbed a visitor while in this dive, whether caught in the act or afterwards identified by the man whose companion she had been, she was compelled to disgorge her booty and could not again enter the place. This in part accounted for its popularity.

Its open violation of the law and the publicity given to it by the suicides committed there marked it as the first to go when a reform administration began its town-cleaning crusade in 1901.

The Palm Garden was another notorious resort closed at the same time. The habitues of this place were a beastly lot of creatures, with whom even the depraved wretches of the Bowery would not consort. There are few public places of this character in this city, for the penalty is heavy and no mercy is shown, as there is no excuse for their bestiality.

The Slide, a resort of this kind, was raided a few years ago and the proprietor spent years in jail, notwithstanding his wealth and political prominence. Afterward the habitues assembled in a dive on Chrystie Street which they called the Palm. When too much publicity was given to this place, the proprietor, "French Lou," moved to a saloon in Fifth Street near the Bowery, known to the police for years as the headquarters of the "Reds" or rabid anarchists. This was then called the "New Palm." Complaints from the tenants of the house compelled the police to close the saloon and the wretches scattered. They now congregate in a clubroom.

After McGurk's Sporting House was closed the other Bowery dives either closed their doors or were conducted so quietly that only regular frequenters knew of their existence. The piano players were discharged, singing and dancing were prohibited, and strangers were not admitted during the prohibited hours (1 to 5 A. M.).

Lynch's White House, near Grand Street, and the Rosedale, near Fifth Street, had apparently sufficient influence to run openly until 1903, when both closed their doors. There are still a number of dives on and near the Bowery, not run under distinctive titles, and all conducted so quietly that they are not known to be dives except by their regular patrons. A glance through the side door, however, will disclose the large room at the end of the hall. One dive just west of the Bowery was conducted under a distinctive title and in the old style until 1906, and in the winter of 1908-1909 several dives and dance halls were opened near Chatham Square.

A saloon still doing business near Catherine Street is the refuge of the old, haggard, tattered wretches, women who have reached the lowest depths of poverty and depravity, who would not be admitted to any other resort. The men who frequent this place are fit mates for the women. The "Flea Bag," on Park Row, is a similar resort. A dive on Mott Street, near Chatham Square, is frequented mainly by opium habitues; the women are younger and more depraved than in the other resorts of this character. The saloon part in these is like the ordinary Bowery morgue, the back room is generally filthy, poorly lighted, and altogether repulsive. Some of these places are the rendezvous for petty thieves and pickpockets of the district.

Places of this character frequently change hands (nominally), the actual proprietor securing a new license under an alias or in the name of the manager or a dummy, whenever a serious complaint is made against him or his place by which his license is forfeited.

The Oxford Hotel is a Raines Law hotel, and was formerly a dive. The saloon part is like the ordinary Bowery corner liquor store. Behind it is a small room reached only from the side street. Here, seated at six tables, was a low type of the Bowery wretch, human harpies whose specialty was drunken sailors. The women were old, ugly and vicious, and no artifice could make them acceptable to a man in his sober senses. Above the room is the hotel to which they took their victims when the latter had reached the state of imbecility. The place was owned by a notorious dive-keeper, but run in the name of another. This and several similar Bowery resorts have recently given up the dive adjunct and announce that they are conducted under a new management, renting rooms to gentlemen only. This is one of the results of an honest police administration. Nearby is one of the few brothel dives left in that vicinity.

Another Oxford on the Bowery is a gaudy saloon where small politicians congregate. Flynn's saloon, corner Pell Street, the headquarters of "Chuck Connors," is a tough liquor store where old rounders are supplied in the back room. Steve Brodie's is at present the best known of the low Bowery saloons.

The Rosedale, recently closed, was another Raines Law hotel and dive. It was frequented by the peripatetic sisterhood, their panders, and some of the former Palm habitues. The reputed manager of this resort has run similar resorts on and near the Bowery for twenty years, each place running a few months and then closed (by the advice of the police?), and a new place under a different name opened nearby. The manager has considerable political weight in the district, and has never been troubled by the police. He has now a Tenderloin resort.

Many of the female frequenters of the Rosedale and similar places in the same locality were women who had just come from the more pretentious Fourteenth Street resorts. There is a gradual downward path for these women. Starting at the fashionable resorts in the Tenderloin, they pass down Sixth Avenue to Fourteenth Street, then down Third Avenue to the Bowery, where, near the upper end, they first reach places like the Rosedale. As they go down they finally reach the tough dives at the lower end of the Bowery and on Park Row.

On Hester Street, not far from the Bowery, is, perhaps, the dirtiest of the Raines Law hotel dives in the district.

What the Bowery morgue is for the men, this place is for the women, a foul liquor-store with a small side room where these depraved creatures can drink whiskey by the tumblerful.

The women are coarse, vile, ugly and old, and rarely succeed in capturing a victim, although their favors can be had for the price of a drink.

If the price of a room in a Raines Law hotel is any criterion of its standing, this one is at the foot, for a room can be had here for 25 cents a night.

On the same street, west of the Bowery, is a similar Raines Law hotel and dive, having a somewhat cleaner saloon.

These two places are not dives as the word is understood on the Bowery, the side or back room being merely an adjunct to the hotel and saloon. Almost every Raines Law hotel on the Bowery has such a side or back room where the preliminaries leading to the engagement of a room up-stairs are made.

The old time dance halls such as were conducted by Harry Hill and Billy McGlory have disappeared from the Bowery. In their stead dancing is sometimes indulged in in the dives. The tables and chairs in the middle of the room are pushed aside, giving a clear space where those present can dance to the music of a piano. There are no square dances, but a waiter calls out, "take partners for a dance," the men ask any of the women to "step up for a turn," and away they whirl. The dance may be a waltz, polka, schottische or galop, the time of the music depending upon the mood of the piano player. All is called "spieling."

After the dance the tables are pushed back and the place becomes a dive again.

The Emerald on Chatham Square is the largest and gaudiest of the dance hall dives.

There are several ballrooms in Povertyville, in which dances are held nightly during the winter, sometimes by respectable parties, sometimes by the vicious, and by fictious clubs.

When not regularly engaged the proprietor of one of these halls hangs a sign on the door announcing that ——————— Social Club will hold its annual ball that evening. No tickets are sold in advance, the admission fee, usually 25 cents, admitting "gent and ladies," being paid on entering. When women come unaccompanied by men they wait before the door until some man without a companion is about to enter. They will either ask him to pass them in or they will follow in his wake as his "ladies." In this way the women of the street get in without paying the admission fee.

There is no printed dance program, a floor manager calling out the dances, the intervals between them being regulated by the number of people drinking at the tables. In the course of the evening women will find companions who will accompany them home or to nearby hotels, and by midnight most of the men are gone. The ball then comes to an end. The proprietor's returns are derived from admission fees, hat checks and drinks sold.

Sometimes a hall is engaged by a dive-keeper or a few sports, who form a temporary club. The tickets are sold or given away, the returns from the hat box covering all expenses. At these balls the women are admitted free, and those who ordinarily seek them at the dives go on such nights to the ball. It is at these affairs that the tough dances so grossly caricatured on the vaudeville stage can be seen. The Bowery tough who attends such balls does not possess a dress suit, high hat, white shirt, cuffs or patent leather pumps. The dress suit can be hired and by basting and pinning can be made to fit. The ordinary colored shirt or a celluloid shirt front takes the place of a white one. Where the shirt front is used the cuffs are pinned to the sleeves of the coat. The tough does not know how to wear a high hat, although one can be hired for twenty-five cents. As for dancing-shoes, his brogans serve him better than pumps. A white collar, a bow or a four-in-hand tie, white or colored, and a rhinestone pin complete his ball outfit. This is, however, only used on state occasions. At the ordinary dances, such as are conducted by the hall proprietor, his ordinary suit, generally the only one he has, is worn. The women have no ball dresses. On special occasions they hire a silk dress or wear a gauzy summer waist, black skirt, and imitation jewelry.

The program consists almost wholly of round dances, these being the most popular with the dancers and most productive of thirst, hence most profitable to the bar. While the women are fairly good dancers as a rule, the men, with few exceptions, know one step, a polka or schottische, rarely a waltz, timing the step to the time of the music or breaking into a galop irrespective of the music. This end galop is the mild prototype of the tough dance of the stage.

While there is less grace there is often more decorum at these dances than at some so-called fashionable balls held in New York every winter.

The saddest feature of these dances is the opportunity they offer working girls of the vicinity to dance. The girls go, are admitted free, and being, as a rule, more attractive than the brazen women of the street, are sought after by the men. Many of the women of the street began their downward career at these balls or soirees, as they are sometimes called.

The Bowery concert-hall is an institution which depends for its existence upon the temper of the police. Under a strict interpretation of the theatrical law the ordinary Bowery concert-hall can not be run profitably, and with an efficient police force carrying out the spirit of the law there are but few concert-halls on the Bowery.

One of these, the Atlantic Garden, has been referred to. In spite of the degeneration of the neighborhood it has maintained its respectability, and is to-day the only place of its kind on the street to which a man can take his wife in safety.

The Casino, a Jewish vaudeville hall, having little to attract the American, was recently closed. The Oriental Music Hall, on Grand Street, and several other similar places are ordinary concert halls, frequented mainly by

Jews. They have nothing to recommend them, and there is little to criticize. They are poor, but not vicious places like the next described hall.

The Lyceum Music Hall represents a type which keeps within the law, but approaches the line of indecency so closely that a man would not take his wife or daughter into it. This type has its stage, dressing rooms, paid performers, and runs under a concert license, but it has also its barker and its bouncer, its persistent waiters, and disreputable women at the tables. Admission is free, but the visitor is expected to drink, and not dally too long over one glass. The orchestra consists of a violin and a piano, the performers are three or four women, who sing and dance at irregular intervals. When visitors enter, a performer is called out to sing or dance. When there are few people in the room the performers do not appear. Their songs are popular airs with variations coarsely suggestive, even to vileness; their dances, the ordinary clog and jig. They are not permitted to appear in costume among the audience, but they convert the stage dress into a street dress in a minute, and then appear on the floor drinking with admirers.

Places of this description do not pay, as those looking for good vaudeville where admission is free and they can drink and smoke, go to the Atlantic Garden or to the resorts further uptown, while those looking for depravity find what they want in the dives.

The typical low Bowery concert-hall can only exist when the most liberal construction is put upon the theatrical law, and the police then refuse to see its evasion and violation. Under the present police administration not one is running on the Bowery, but as soon as the word is passed out that there will be no police interference, they spring up over night. A manager who has the proper kind of influence hires a large store, covers the windows with flaring theatrical posters, and announces that a concert hall will be opened the next day.

A few boards placed upon a couple of carpenter's horses at the further end of the store form the stage. A screen at the side of the stage is the makeshift for a dressing room, and a larger screen placed near the door hides the interior from the gaze of the passerby. A piano, a score or more of tables and twice as many chairs are hired and put in during the day. A bar and an ice box are placed near the entrance or in the cellar. The piano goes near the stage. An electric light within, a gas bracket with colored globes and a billboard covered with theatrical posters outside, complete the equipment of the place. The glassware, screens, stage, outside gas bracket and billboard must be paid for immediately, the other things are hired.

All these are secured and put in place within a few hours after the store is rented. When such places are allowed to exist there is no difficulty in securing an excise and a concert license.

The help necessary are a manager, a "barker," who stands before the door shouting its attractions, a "bouncer," whose principal duty is to throw out undesirable visitors, a few waiters, and the professor, a poor devil who is willing to thump the piano for fifty cents a night.

The bouncer is usually a pugilist obtained from a sporting resort, the others are secured from the lodging-houses. The talent consists of some of the women of the street, and sometimes a waiter, all volunteers. The supply far exceeds the demand, for it gives the women a chance to appear on the stage, and they thereafter call themselves actresses, and it brings them prominently before the public in the place, with the greater opportunity of securing patrons from among the audience. There is generally a stock costume, furnished by the manager, which each woman dons before she goes on the stage. She must go on in costume and, as few of these women have any other wardrobe but that which they wear on the street, they must accommodate themselves to the sleeveless waist and the short skirt furnished by the house. Whether tall or short, stout or lean, all wear the same costume. The singer's popularity depends upon the character of her songs, and the more vulgar they are the more she is applauded. What is, however, of more importance to her than applause is to find admirers who will invite her to drink, as she gets commissions on the drinks they order.

If one can be induced to order champagne at three dollars a bottle, her commission is a dollar. The stuff furnished is a special brand of champagne cider costing thirty cents a bottle. On wines and liquors she receives twenty per cent; on beer nothing. Her own drink is usually sherry at twenty-five cents a glass. There is sometimes an understanding between the women and the manager whereby they are not charged for drinks they order. If a party who appear to be liberal spenders enter, one of the women will sit at the table and invite them to drink with her. They accept the invitation and offer to treat in return. She accepts, orders champagne and they dare not refuse.

The lovers of the women who frequent the concert halls are not tolerated there, as they spend nothing, and occupy seats with the women which might be occupied by more profitable patrons. Sightseers are always welcome, as they usually spend something and do not remain long.

When such disreputable concert halls are permitted to exist they are virtually under police protection, and while the visitor is safe as long as he remains sober and pays in small change, should he be robbed he has no redress, for complaint to the police will be unavailing. Nor is it safe to quarrel with a woman or a waiter, for both are protected by the bouncer, and the policeman on post is the latter's friend.

The presence or absence of these mushroom concert halls on the Bowery is an unfailing gauge of the political status of the city. Under a reform administration and with an energetic police commissioner who is independent of politics, such resorts disappear. This was the condition of the Bowery in 1887, in 1895 when President Roosevelt was police commissioner, in 1902 when General Greene was at the head of the police department, and even at present with a Tammany administration and an independent, liberal minded, energetic police commissioner the Bowery is free from these openly vicious resorts.

While these public haunts of vice have disappeared or are under cover, there are a number of places where vice flourishes, but only the initiated may enter.

There are gambling-houses, poolrooms, opium joints, brothels and private clubs where interdicted vices are practiced so quietly that only regular patrons know of their existence.

There is also a form of disreputable joint which keeps within the letter of the law, though violating its spirit; but being run mainly by Germans and Hungarians, for these nationalities are little known. These are the "cider rooms" and "coffee rooms," found east of the Bowery. Some of the coffee rooms are simply gambling houses where "Stuss," a Hungarian gambling game, and poker are played. Coffee is furnished instead of whiskey.

In most of the coffee rooms having waitresses, and in the cider rooms, almost without exception, the sale of coffee or cider is a blind. The waitresses are for hire, the proprietor having a flat behind the store or nearby, to which patrons are conducted after the preliminaries have been arranged over the cup of coffee or glass of cider.

These places are run without excise license, and when liquor is called for the proprietor will offer to go to the corner liquor store and buy some for the patron. In this way he circumvents the law, although the liquor really comes from bottles in his ice box.

These places are rarely interfered with by the police.

We hear occasionally of "knock-out" drops in the Bowery saloons. Knock-out drops is a solution of chloral hydrate, the pungent taste of which is immediately noticed by a person in his sober senses. In almost every case where it was used the victim came into the saloon partly intoxicated, drank with a stranger at the bar, and then accompanied the stranger to a private room or office in the saloon. The victim receives the drug in a drink furnished by the bartender. In his befuddled condition he does not notice the taste, and in a few minutes becomes drowsy and falls into a deep sleep. In this condition he is robbed, and as soon as he shows signs of returning consciousness, he is led to the door and pushed out. He will, as a rule, walk a short distance, then lie down, still drowsy, and sleep. He is picked up by the police, and the next morning the story is in the press. A bartender will never give the drug unless the victim is in the hands of the accomplice and away from the bar. Stertorous breathing shows the bartender that he has given the man an overdose, and no time is lost in getting the victim out through the hall or side entrance and left on the street.

Knock-out drops are supplied in half dram vials, each vial containing 20 grains of chloral, a vial full being used at a time.

Bartenders in saloons frequented by the criminal classes generally know what the drug is and have no difficulty in obtaining it. It is, however, rarely used in the Bowery saloons, as the risk is too great and the prospects of making a haul too small. Most of the reported cases of knock-out drops on the Bowery are simply cases of robbery while drunk.

Gambling is the most persistent pastime indulged in in Povertyville, and to thousands in the district it is the only source of livelihood. Poker, policy, and crap shooting are the principal forms of gambling practiced. There is one place on the Bowery known to every Bowery sport, having the more elaborate paraphernalia required in faro, rouge et noir and roulette, although rumor has it that these games are also played in some of the private clubs in the district.

There is a gambling house which has been running for years without police interruption. The window shutters on a level with the elevated railroad structure are never opened, and no gleam from the gas lights burning day and night within ever reaches the outside. The place is over a liquor store frequented by small sports, and is reached only through a hall leading from the back room. There is an emergency exit leading to a store on a side street. In the large room over the store is a faro layout and a few poker tables for private parties.

Although the place is probably known by the police, complaints never reach them, as strangers are not admitted unless vouched for by a frequenter, and the games are honestly conducted. This is, however, not due to moral scruples, but because the players are expert gamblers and know all the tricks of the game. The place is frequented by small sports, politicians and merchants with sporting or gambling proclivities. In its favor it may be said that the proprietor will not allow confidence men to use the place in carrying out their schemes.

Another game was opened over a saloon run by an ex-convict. Its frequenters were mainly of the criminal classes, and no one could enter who was not personally known to the proprietor. It is said that the police permitted this place to run, as it enabled them to locate suspects through stool-pigeons who played there. When complaints came that confidence men were making their headquarters there the police ordered the place closed. (The stool-pigeons are ex-convicts who continue their associations with the criminal classes and sell whatever information they can pick up to the police. Occasionally they are engaged by the police to obtain information in special cases.)

The policy shops are now conducted so quietly that it is difficult to locate them. Since the crusade began by Captain Goddard and the Anti-Policy Society these places, formerly run as openly as dives and gambling houses, have disappeared, and at present there is not a regular policy shop on the Bowery. Those who still play the game go to a cigar store near the Bowery, where they meet a runner or agent for a policy shop. He receives their money and gives them a slip for the cap, saddle, gig or horse, as the various combinations of numbers played are called. After the afternoon drawing, which was supposed to take place in Kentucky, but which has been shown to take place in this city, the runner again appears in the store to pay the winners. Poolrooms, where bets are made on horse races, open and shut as the police will. The Bowery is practically clear of them at the present moment, but it is safe to say that this is only a temporary condition. With a lenient police captain in any one of the five precincts bordering on the Bowery, poolrooms spring up in that precinct. A large room is hired, one side is partitioned off, and in the larger space where the bettors congregate, a number of blackboards are set up. These blackboards contain the names of the horses in each race and the betting odds given at the race track. Behind the partition is a telegraph or telephone receiver, from which one of the employes reads aloud the progress of each race as it is run, and announces the winner. The bettors place their money through a wicket in the partition and receive a pool ticket giving the name of the horse and the amount bet. The winning tickets are redeemed through this or through an adjoining wicket. Pool selling, as this form of gambling is called, is a violation of the law, but to convict the bookmaker or pool seller it is necessary that he be identified as the person receiving the money. To prevent such identification a shade or cover is placed over the wicket in such a way that only the hand of the person receiving the money and handing out the pool ticket can be seen.

Most of the betting on the races now done on the Bowery is through handbooks—that is, through bookmakers who have no poolrooms but accept bets at the poolroom odds, and pay winnings as the returns come over the ticker of the saloon where they make their headquarters. Bets are also made through "turf commissioners" or agents, who place bets at the track or in poolrooms further up town. Some of these agents are honest, and actually go to the track or poolrooms to place the bets entrusted to them, but most are bookmakers risking their own money, with the additional advantage over regular bookmakers of charging for each bet they make and receiving, besides, a commission of the winnings of their patrons. When the small bookmaker finds that he would lose heavily in the settlement of bets he "welches," or disappears, with the stakes. When the "turf commissioner," who risks his own money against the patron's bets, instead of placing the bets at the track, finds he would lose heavily he returns the patron's wagers, with the plausible excuse that the poolroom was raided or that he was sick. He is then considered an honest turf commissioner.

On June 16th, 1903, the only poolroom then running on the Bowery was raided by the police. It was supposed to be run by a member of a well-known family of politicians, and had been doing business less than a week. From a window in the room a heavy rope was stretched to the extension of a nearby theater, and a ladder led from the extension to a yard in Chrystie Street. The manager and his employees escaped this way.

Since the passage of the race-track betting law by the New York State Legislature in 1908, horse racing has declined in this State, and interest in horse-race betting has virtually ceased in the Bowery district. During the summer months there is some illicit betting on races held near the city, but there was no poolroom on the Bowery in the summer of 1908 or since then.

The club rooms are the only resorts where the vicious are free from police molestation.

While many of the clubs in Povertyville are places of recreation for the working men, and as such are commendable, some were organized to evade a badly tinkered excise law, while others were started by the vicious classes to give them a place where, under cover of the law, they could drink, gamble, and plan nefarious projects.

One of the most notorious of the last class is a club in Doyer Street, near the Bowery. The lower part of the ramshackle club house is occupied by a liquor store run by one of the club members. The upper part is used for club purposes, a large room being used as a club room, sitting room, and dance hall, while smaller rooms are used by card parties. The membership consists mainly of the vile, vicious and criminal classes, but there are also enrolled others who have business relations with the law breakers. The business affairs of the club are conducted in an orderly manner, but at its social affairs orgies are carried on as far as the police will permit. At the annual balls given by the club there are collected the largest number of criminals outside of prison. The women present are almost without exception the mistresses of the men, criminals like their partners, or women of the street.

This is an incorporated club. There are several such incorporated clubs in the district, the sole object of which seems to be to afford a place to gamble under cover of the law or a place of refuge when evading its penalty. There are also many clubs not incorporated, having rooms in rear houses, in cellars, stables, and other out of the way places. Such resorts are the "hang-outs" or headquarters of the gangs of toughs who infest the district.

Sometimes they call themselves a club and elect a president, invariably the one who has committed the most hazardous crime. More often they prefer to call themselves "the gang," prefixing what they consider a euphonious title, and they follow a self-appointed leader, whose only claim to leadership rests upon his willingness to fight anyone who disputes his title. In the tenements and shanties which covered the area now embraced by Mulberry Bend Park, a little west of the Bowery, there were scores of such hang outs, until the city authorities wiped out this, the most vicious block in the city, and perhaps in the world. In the middle of the block, back of the houses fronting on Mulberry and Baxter Streets, were a number of old buildings occupied by rag pickers, beggars and criminals. These houses were reached from the houses in front, by alleys which led to the streets, and by cross-alleys and back yards. If an escaping criminal succeeded in reaching one of these alleys he was safe, for it was impossible to determine in which direction he went after he had reached the first cross-alley, and every house was a refuge. From the Bandits' Roost, a house near the center of the block, the name of which well indicated its character, Mulberry Street in front, two alleys and two adjoining buildings could be reached, while a cellar communicated with the cellar of a house back of a house on Baxter Street. The Bandits' Roost and several other buildings on the block were the dens of criminals. On the ground floor of one of these rear buildings a gang had fitted up two rooms as club rooms and headquarters, with spoils gathered in their raids. Lace curtains covered windows which were never cleaned. A carpet lay on the floor of the two rooms, the unused portion of the roll lying in the smaller room, forming a head-rest. The carpet was littered with cigar stumps and ashes, torn playing cards, broken clay pipes, etc. A kitchen table covered with green cloth, probably the cover of a billiard table, and a number of beer kegs used as chairs, comprised the furniture. On the mantlepiece were a lot of bric-a-brac, cards, slates, pieces of chalk and beer glasses. The back room was filled with clothing, bundles and bags, the proceeds of thefts, while some of the gang lay on the floor smoking or dozing. One of these was badly battered in a fight for leadership. This place was a typical thieves' den. Another such den existed in Elizabeth Street, one block west of the Bowery.

A number of gangs have gained considerable notoriety during the past few years on account of their frequent encounters with the police and the feuds among themselves. They are really not as formidable as press accounts would indicate. The personnel of the gang consists of a leader who gives his name to the gang, a few vicious friends and some half-grown boys, viciously inclined, who try to emulate the others in vice. They have no organization, no headquarters, nothing more than a favorite "hang-out" where the leader meets his friends and discusses crimes with them. The leader has generally some political influence whereby he attracts criminals and would-be criminals who will do his bidding on election day, and who look to him for aid when they come in conflict with the police. **When the leader** is sent to prison the gang disintegrates.

The chief occupations of the members of these gangs are petty thievery and gambling. Sometimes they fight among themselves and occasionally a member is killed in a feud or by members of his **own gang, if he** is suspected of being a stool pigeon.

CHAPTER V

HAUNTS AND HOMES.

EVEN wretches must live, they must have shelter and food, and Povertyville supplies them with both.

Those with means, honestly or ill-gotten, are never at a loss; not so, however, the poor devil who is not a criminal, who has no home, friends or money. His waking hours can be spent in the streets, saloons, dives, missions and reading rooms. But he needs some place where he can rest, forget and dream, sheltered from storm and cold. For the respectable woman, so situated, private philanthropy has amply provided. The penniless man, however, who will not steal, must beg enough to pay for a night's lodging or must beg for a lodging at one of the Salvation Army hotels or go to the Municipal lodging house. If he has good recommendations he can remain a few days at the Bowery branch of the Young Men's Christian Association, and if he shows a willingness to work the Charity Organization Society will provide for him. The Industrial Christian Alliance in Bleecker Street maintains a temporary home for destitute men who are willing to work at brush making, carpentering, shoemaking or tailoring until other work is

SITTING ROOM OF BOWERY LODGING HOUSE.

provided. If the destitute fellow will not avail himself of one, of these places, he can rest on the Park benches, on trucks or in cellars in summer, and in the winter in the comfort houses for men in the parks.

The saloon offers him shelter if he will do the menial work about the place, sweeping floors, cleaning windows, washing cuspidors, etc.

In some saloons the patrons who spend their money over the bar are permitted to remain at night in the back room, while one saloon gives each patron a coupon with each drink, six coupons entitling him to a free bed. In one saloon the back room is crowded nightly. Its patrons, mainly longshoremen and dock workers, earn fair wages, which are spent here for beer and liquor. The generous proprietor, who has grown wealthy from this trade, furnishes them with a plentiful supply of bread, cheese and corned beef, and when their money is gone he permits them to sleep on the chairs and benches in the back room.

For those who can pay there is every grade of hotel and lodging house, from the fairly good Occidental Hotel, where rooms cost a dollar or more a night, to the Park Row lodging houses, in some of which a tramp may lie on the bare floor near the stove for five cents a night. The term hotel implies a more pretentious establishment than the lodging house, and should include a dining room, but many ordinary lodging houses on the Bowery bear the names of hotels. The law does not clearly define the difference between hotel and lodging house, and there is a conflict between the requirements of a hotel under the Raines law and under the sanitary and building codes. The Raines law demands ten bedrooms, a kitchen and dining room. The building code demands fifteen rooms. The sanitary code demands 400 cubic feet of space for each guest and a window in each sleeping apartment, opening upon an air shaft, court, street or open space. Under this rule a hotel cannot have more bedrooms than it has windows, while a lodging house may have a dormitory with as many guests as the cubic space will allow under the 400 cubic foot rule. The "private rooms" in the cheap lodging houses are not legally bedrooms, but portions of the main room with the partitions between the beds. The partitions between the "rooms" do not extend to the ceiling, as that would make them legally bedrooms, violating the sanitary code. Wire network extends over the top of the partitions, instead of a ceiling, to prevent guests from making surreptitious visits to their neighbors' rooms when the latter are out.

There is, besides these, that vicious anomaly, the **Raines Law Hotel**, which will be described later.

The best and most unique of the lodging houses in this section are the two Mills Hotels, number one in Bleecker Street, with 1550 rooms, number two in Rivington Street, with 600 rooms. Both are under the same management and conducted alike. (A third Mills Hotel was recently opened.)

The rooms, costing 20 cents a night, are small and plain but clean and neat. These hotels contain large reading rooms, smoking lobbies, barber shops and laundries, and the guests have the usual hotel conveniences, including elevator, steam heat and electric light. They are legally hotels, not lodging houses.

Restaurants connected with these hotels supply good, wholesome food at very low prices, and are patronized by hundreds who are not hotel guests.

These two hotels are patronized by a class distinct from the Bowery lodging house patrons. They are mostly men working for small salaries, self-respecting men who desire clean and refined surroundings so far as limited means can secure refinement. They do not come under the heading of Povertyville's wretches. For a short time in 1904 and 1905 a number of broken-down sports and gamblers made their home here, but the manager soon turned them out. In the better class of Bowery lodging houses, the rates are from 25 to 50 cents a night. The highest priced rooms face the street, have carpets and curtains, and the ordinary hotel room furnishings, bed, wash-stand, mirror, chair and bureau. The cheapest are on an upper floor, face the yard or court, are smaller than the other, have muslin window shades, and oilcloth on the floor, otherwise they are furnished like the other rooms. These lodging houses—some are called hotels— have sitting rooms, and most have free baths. In the lodging houses charging from 15 to 35 cents a night the best rooms are furnished like the best rooms in the better class lodging houses. There is, however, a general air of povery about them more noticeable than in the cheapest rooms in the better lodging houses.

The cheapest rooms, or stalls, as the lodgers call them, are mere closets about 8 feet long and 5 feet wide, partitioned off the sides of a long hall or room, with a passage way between the two rows of closets or "private rooms." Each room has a bed or cot, a stool, and sometimes a washstand.

Where there is a washstand there is a tin basin and a pitcher. If there is no washstand in the room, there is a common lavatory at the end of the hall, and adjoining it is a closet where the lodgers may take a shower bath.

There is usually a sitting room, poorly lighted, with benches instead of chairs, where lodgers often sit through hot summer nights.

Some of these lodging houses have drying rooms where lodgers may wash and dry their clothing, and most have a washstand at the end of the hall, where, to the faucets, are attached by chains a comb, hair brush, and whisk broom.

In the poorest lodging houses where the rates are from 10 to 25 cents, rooms are closets like the closets of other lodging houses. These hold either cots or old-fashioned beds. Where cots are used the bedding consists of a sheet thrown over the bed, a straw pillow and a blanket. In the old-style beds there is in addition a straw mattress, so thin, however, that an uneasy sleeper generally arises with the marks of the bed slats on his body.

For ten or fifteen cents the lodger receives a cot in a dormitory holding from twenty to a hundred beds. In a lodging house near Park Row bunks were formerly used instead of beds; the boards forming the bunk were held up by short posts or boxes, one row of bunks being above the other.

Each bunk accommodated two sleepers. The bed consisted of a lot of straw, covered by a piece of canvas, a canvas bag filled with straw formed a pillow, and a horse blanket covered all. No objection was made to dirt or vermin. The lodgers rarely removed their clothing, but shoes were removed out of consideration for the shins of their bed fellows. Late-comers who could not obtain a bunk lay on the floor, paying five cents for the privilege.

In some lodging houses double-decker bunks, having one row of beds above the other, are still used.

In the ten-cent lodging house there is a common lavatory, and a spray pan is attached to the faucet by a long rubber tube so that those who wish may take a shower bath. This is seldom used. The common towel is changed when the last white spot disappears, and the comb and brush which are chained to the faucet do service while a few teeth and hair remain.

There is a sitting room with a few benches and a desk near the door, where the clerk receives the dimes and pennies from the guests as they slink in. He enters their names on the register, and assigns each to his bed. In a few moments the lodger has kicked off his shoes, and a moment later his snores join the chorus. Late-comers sit around the stove or lie on the floor. Such are the poorest of the lodging houses.

The lodging houses from Grand Street northward are better than those southward. The poorest are on Park Row and in the side streets. The largest of the poor lodging houses is a six-story building in Mulberry Street, near Park Row. It stands in the rear of some old tenement houses, and is reached through a narrow alley between two houses. Some of these poor lodging houses furnish coffee and rolls, others give tickets good for tobacco or beer.

The new hotel at Chatham Square conducted by the Salvation Army is the largest lodging house in the city with the exception of the Mills Hotel number one.

It has dormitories and small rooms, with rates from fifteen to fifty cents a night. It is equipped with elevators, steam heat, electric lights, spring beds, free baths, etc., and in its conveniences is far in advance of other lodging houses charging the same rates.

But while the inmates pay as much as they would in other lodging houses there is a lack of independence, or rather, there is a sense of dependence upon a philanthropy, a sense or sentiment entirely absent in the guests of the Mills hotels. This may account for the difference in the class of guests at the two hotels.

The old lodging houses of the Salvation Army do not differ except in neatness from the ordinary cheap Bowery lodging houses.

The dormitory of the Bowery branch of the Y. M. C. A. is the most attractive of the Bowery lodging houses. The lodgers are mostly young men in search of work. A charge of fifteen cents is made, but a man without means, having good references and showing a willingness to work, can obtain lodging and meals free until work is secured. As a philanthropic institution this has done more good than any other institution of a similar character in New York.

The guests are aided to obtain positions, religious instincts are fostered, and self-respect is upheld. They are not thrown in contact with the lazy, shiftless, often depraved wretches found in other lodging houses, nor are they obliged to give hypocritical statements about their willingness to be converted and reform in order to obtain a free bed.

The homeless and penniless fellow who cannot obtain a free bed at the Y. M. C. A. or at one of the Salvation Army hotels, can go to the Charity Organization Society in East Twenty-Second Street, where he can obtain lodging and meals if he is willing to do a few hours' work in the wood yard.

As a last resort, he can go to the Municipal lodging house in First Avenue, near 23rd Street. Here are 317 beds, 270 for men, and 47 for women, about one-half being occupied nightly, except in winter, when the place is overcrowded. A new Municipal lodging house holding 1,000 beds was recently opened in 25th Street.

The wretches arrive about 6 P. M., and their names and addresses are entered on the register. Each one is asked how he supports himself, how much money he has about him, and what references he has. Vagrants and those who apply more than three nights in succession are sent to the police station, the others are examined by a physician who excludes those who are suffering from contagious diseases. These are sent to Bellevue Hospital; the others assemble in a large room, where each receives a cup of coffee and a piece of bread. After depositing with the Superintendent whatever of value he may have about him, the applicant receives a numbered bag, and is conducted to the bath room. Here he puts his clothing in the bag, hands it to an attendant and receives a check therefor, and a night shirt. After a shower bath he is assigned to a bed in one of the dormitories. All are awakened at six in the morning, and the bags containing their clothing are returned. The clothing has been subjected to a disinfecting process during the night, and comes back damp and crumpled. This is the general complaint of all who spend a night in the Municipal lodging house.

After dressing, coffee and bread are again served, the inmates are set to work cleaning up the place and at half-past six the men are discharged. The women leave half an hour later. All are easily recognized in the neighborhood by the damp, crumpled appearance of their clothing.

In cold and stormy weather the hours are not strictly adhered to and when the number of applicants exceeds the sleeping accommodations a man's dormitory is turned over to the women, while the men are sent to the pier of the Department of Charities, where cots are put up for them. When the number exceeds the accommodations at the lodging house and pier late comers go on board the city steamboats which tie up at the pier, or are sent to the police station, where they find shelter but little comfort in the unoccupied cells.

Little need be said of the saloons where men are permitted to sleep on chairs or on casks. The men are drunkards who have spent their last cent at the bar and, partly overcome by liquor, they drop into the chairs or on casks and sleep there until they are thrown out in the morning.

There is still one place where the homeless wretches may find shelter, a place to which only the most abject of wretches resort. The writer saw a number of them standing asleep in the toilet room for men in Mulberry Bend Park at 2 A. M. on a February morning in 1908.

The temperature outside was 16 degrees above zero; in the room it was 60 degrees. The wretches here dread the bath in the municipal lodging house, they dare not go to the police station where they would be held as vagrants, which means that most horrible combination—work and wash; they cannot obtain admission to any other free lodging house, and they prefer to spend their last dime for a drink rather than for a bed.

The Raines Law hotels are not intended for permanent guests or all-night patrons. The rooms are rarely occupied for more than an hour or two at a time, the guests slinking in through the side door with their temporary "wives," the "wife" appearing with several "husbands" in succession the same night. The room for which a dollar is charged contains a bed, a chair and a washstand. The bedding is insufficient, the lighting is poor and there is altogether a lack of conveniences as a standing invitation to vacate the room as soon as possible.

No respectable person stops at a hotel of this character, but the female wretches who bring their patrons to them are usually permitted to occupy a room free. This description fits the ordinary Bowery Raines Law hotel of the brothel variety. Some hotels established under this law are in so far respectable that they are conducted as good hotels, furnishing the usual hotel conveniences, yet some of these, notwithstanding their apparent respectability, are patronized almost exclusively by disreputable women and their temporary husbands.

Unfortunately there is no sharp dividing line between the clean, respectable hotel and the ordinary Raines Law house. The mere presence of disreputable persons in a hotel does not necessarily imply that the hotel is disreputable, for such persons can be found even in ultra-fashionable houses. When, however, couple after couple enter a hotel without baggage, not even a hand satchel, register as coming from some distant place and leave the hotel in a few hours, especially when the register shows that none of these couples remain longer than a day, it is safe to assume that the hotel belongs to the Raines Law brothel variety.

While it may appease the vanity of the lawmaker to whose efforts these public brothels owe their existence, it is a disgrace to the legislature which called them into life and to the city of New York which must recognize them as having a legal right to exist.

Not all the so-called hotels operating under the vicious Raines Law are brothels. This law demands that a hotel shall have not less than ten rooms, each containing a bed, for the accommodation of guests. It gives hotel keepers some privileges not possessed by saloon keepers, principally the right to furnish liquors to guests on Sundays. As the Sunday trade in many saloons far exceeds the week-day trade, the saloon keeper hires a floor or two floors over the saloon, places ten cots or folding beds in as many rooms and secures a hotel license. If he has fitted up the rooms merely to comply with the law under which he has secured the license, and has no intention of renting them, an applicant for a room is told that all the rooms are occupied or that the rate for a room is ten dollars a night. The rooms are occupied by the family of the proprietor and his employes, each one registering as a guest. Thus the letter of the law is obeyed and the saloon keeper may sell liquor on Sunday. (The law says liquor may be furnished "with meals," and a legal decision makes a cracker a meal.)

Some of the lodging houses have a distinctive class of patrons. In one of these there are many men of education and refinement who have come down through drink or who seek to hide their identity in Povertyville. However great their efforts to appear other than they really are by mingling with the low and depraved, sooner or later they drift into this place, where they find congenial company. There is little social intercourse among the guests, each respecting the reticence of the others, none seeking to impose or obtain confidence. Sometimes when several are under the influence of liquor, they become loquacious, and will discuss literature, the arts and sciences. Perhaps an allusion will bring to one of the party some bitter memory. He leaves the others and all understand why. To each is brought back the realization of his own position and they separate, each going to his room reflectively.

Another lodging house is known for its frequent brawls. Most of its patrons belong to that class of indigenous wretches who have no moral compunction about cracking a stranger's skull or rifling a neighbor's pockets.

Shortly before election day this place is filled with tramps who lodge here free until they have performed their duty as citizens on election day. They are thrown out the next day.

In another lodging house may be found a number of broken-down theatrical men and sports suffering from dipsomania. (They have the same right to call their vice by a euphonious medical term as the drunkards of uppertendom.) There is more social intercourse among the patrons of this place than in any other lodging house on the street. Heavy gambling is constantly going on, if one judges from the conversation, but buttons take the place of chips, these being sold at ten for a cent, each button representing a dollar.

In one lodging house there are many newcomers from rural districts, probably attracted by the name of the house. It does not differ from the other lodging houses.

It is not until we reach the meanest of the lodging houses that we find that incongruous company composed of all manners and conditions of men, men once accustomed to the high hat and dress suit, men accustomed from infancy to rags, men familiar with the classics and men who cannot spell their names, the whilom master of men and his most servile dependent—men once, wretches now.

While the vicious and penniless go to the lonely rooms and dormitories of the lodging houses, few professional criminals are found there. These as a rule occupy furnished rooms with their paramours, or several such couples may occupy a flat and live together as a free-love community.

The men who are the panders of the women of the street invariably hire a furnished room on or near the Bowery, but the criminals and thugs prefer a flat where, with their mistresses, thieves like themselves, they live in comfort. Sometimes three such couples take a flat together, one posing as man and wife, the latter having a sister and a servant with her. The other two men show up later as boarders. They live quietly, pay their rent promptly, do not interfere with other tenants, and, although suspicion may be aroused by the irregular hours at which the members arrive and depart, they remain until they run afoul of the police.

Private philanthropy has done more for the fallen and disreputable woman than for the homeless and penniless woman who tries to maintain her honor and her self-respect.

For the latter class there are four places where they can obtain free lodgings. At the "Free Home for Young Girls," in East 11th Street, girls between the ages of 13 and 25 are provided with a temporary home, until situations can be secured for them in Christian families.

In the Shelter for Respectable Girls, East 46th Street, Protestant working women can find a temporary home. In the Bowery district is the St. Barnabas House in Mulberry Street. Here destitute women without regard to race, creed or color, are kept a few days. Whites and blacks, Americans, Italians, Russians, the old and the young, receive equal care and attention, a very laudable provision from a philanthropic standpoint, although very distasteful to a high-spirited American girl in adversity. Such a girl rarely remains more than a day in this home. She will then go to one of the other homes if she can obtain admission. As a final resort the destitute woman can go to the Municipal lodging house. Here she is thrown in contact with the most wretched of her class.

The Salvation Army has a lodging house for women, on the Bowery, where the rates are ten to fifteen cents, but penniless women can sometimes obtain lodgings free.

For respectable women who can pay a little, there are a number of homes where rates are from 15 cents upwards a night. On the Bowery itself there is the Salvation Army lodging house, a worthy philanthropy in its way, lacking, however, the elevating influence of refined surroundings and company.

In Rivington Street, near the Bowery, is a woman's lodging house conducted like the better class of men's lodging houses, with rooms from 15 to 50 cents a night.

There are a number of temporary homes for respectable women where low rates are charged and home comforts are furnished.

These are all semi-philanthropic, the income for board and lodging being insufficient to cover the running expenses, the deficiency being made up by voluntary contributions.

Those within a short distance of the Bowery are the Florence Hotel in East 14th Street, the homes conducted by the Ladies' Christian Union, one in 9th Street near Broadway, the other in 2nd Avenue near 18th Street, and the Margaret Louise Home in East 16th Street. This last is connected with the Y. W. C. A.

The ordinary woman of the street generally hires a furnished room in a side street near the Bowery where a number of houses are occupied exclusively by women of this class. The rooms are poorly furnished, muslin shades, oil cloth, a bed, wash-stand, bureau and chair comprising the entire contents of the room.

Occasionally one will hire a flat in a respectable house, furnish it, and live there with her lover as husband and wife; or an old woman will hire a flat and let out rooms to these women, who pose as her daughters.

The tenement house commissioners are making strenuous efforts to drive such women out of respectable tenements. In one house on 2nd Street a woman who hired a flat for herself and two daughters was dispossessed two months later when the family of "daughters" had increased to nine.

While a wretch is still attractive she can always earn enough to hire a furnished room. Later, when she must depend upon the drunken fellow who cannot see straight, she falls back upon a Raines Law hotel, to which she conducts him. Still later, when not even the drunken sailor will consort with her and she must do washing and scrubbing, with occasional stealing, her nights are spent in the back rooms of the lowest dives. Then comes the Salvation Army, the Municipal lodging house, the police station and the workhouse. Only as a last resort will the woman of the street apply at a home for fallen women. On the rare occasions when a woman of this class becomes conscience-stricken, she will apply to be committed to a reformatory institution. Even then she is likely to change her mind before entering. As a rule when these women apply at a home for fallen women it is to obtain shelter for a few days and perhaps some clothing.

The Florence Crittenton Mission in Bleecker Street near the Bowery, the Washington Square Home for Friendless Girls on Washington Square South, and the Salvation Army Industrial Home in East 15th Street are the ones to which these women usually apply.

Here they receive board and lodging and such mental, moral and industrial training as would fit them to become respected working women. All this training is, however, wasted on most of them, for they are unaccustomed to mental or manual labor and do not take kindly to either. In a few days after they leave they are in their old haunts again, looking for customers.

There are several reformatories and homes for fallen women to which such women are committed by police magistrates and which receive fallen women who apply voluntarily. Few, however, go voluntarily to what they consider a prison. Young women who want to give up their vicious vocation prefer to go to the Washington Square Home, which does not lay special stress in its name or methods upon religion or a religious denomination. Older women generally go to one of the Salvation Army homes. A few are attracted by the street services of the Florence Crittenton Mission and go to the Mission House, which is a short distance from the Bowery.

Brothels were once as numerous in Povertyville as the Raines Law hotels are now. Before determined efforts were made to stamp them out, and while men of means still visited the Bowery district for their pleasures, there were scores of unobtrusive, small buildings just east of the Bowery, where "madams" and their girls were housed. There was nothing to indicate their character to the passer-by, and frequently the dwellers in adjoining houses knew nothing of their neighbors. In these houses the basement was used as a dining room and kitchen, the parlor was the reception room where the girls sat awaiting their patrons. The upper rooms were bedrooms. When it became necessary to attract patrons a cigar store was opened in the basement or on the ground floor.

When a stranger entered, madam would sell him a cigar, if that was his purpose, but would suggest that he visit the reception room upstairs. As the class of patrons became poorer, the number of disreputable houses decreased. Instead of these, there are now the cider rooms and a few cigar stores having rooms in the rear or over the store.

The brothels of the eighties were the prototypes of the fashionable houses of ill fame later found in the Tenderloin district. The few remaining in Povertyville today are poor in their furnishings, repellant in their surroundings and in constant danger of being raided by the police. It is safe to say that the "Ladies Boarding House," as it was known for forty years, will soon be extinct in Povertyville.

On a few blocks east of the Bowery, in what was known as the Red Light district, there are still a few houses of this character. The Red Light district was so called because the hall light in disreputable houses had a red globe or shone through red curtains covering the transom of the hall door. A red light before a cigar store, cider room or coffee room indicated its purpose. The Parisian licensed brothel has a red lantern with the number of the house over the door. The few remaining houses of this character in the district have no distinguishing marks other than the women who sometimes stand before the door to attract patrons. The best known has had its liquor license revoked and now admits only habitues.

In Chrystie Street is a beggar's colony where a score or more of these wretches congregate in four small rooms of a rear house. Here they sleep, eat, gamble and quarrel. One room is the kitchen, dining room and sitting room, the others are sleeping apartments, The wretches pay 50 cents a week for the privilege of sleeping on the floor and 25 cents more for a cup of coffee and a half loaf of bread in the morning.

The beggar colonies are constantly on the move, as they are in violation of the sanitary code and house owners turn them out when they find for what purpose the rooms are used.

A colony of old wretches who hang about street corners on the East Side was recently turned out of a ramshackle house in Oliver Street. They slept upon mattresses laid upon the floor, paying five or ten cents a night for the privilege.

The question of food is more readily solved by wretches than that of lodgings.

For those who can pay there is every grade of restaurant from Lorber's restaurant on Grand Street near the Bowery, and the restaurant of the Occidental Hotel, which compare favorably with good restaurants on

Broadway, to the miserable hole on Roosevelt Street, where one and two cent meals are furnished. The St. Andrews Coffee Stands, supported by private charity, furnish one-cent meals—either coffee, soup or beans.

Besides the regular restaurants there are saloons having lunch counters, where a small charge is made for meals, saloons furnishing meals at the noon hour, the free-lunch counters, the meals furnished by missions as an inducement to the wretches to attend the services, and two charities, private enterprises, which furnish food free to the hungry without making public appeals, and without hiring brass bands and reporters.

In Lyon's restaurant, the largest on the Bowery, as elaborate a meal can be obtained as in good restaurants elsewhere. The prices are somewhat higher than in other restaurants on the Bowery, but much lower than the prices charged for the same quality and quantity of food in fashionable restaurants. Of course, the service and surroundings in a Bowery restaurant do not compare with what we expect to find on the Avenue or Broadway.

In Lorber's restaurant the meals furnished are as good and plentiful as are furnished in uptown establishments, and the prices are about one-third less.

Of the cheaper restaurants, those connected with the Mills hotels furnish perhaps the best meals for the price. They charge ten cents for breakfast consisting of a cup of coffee, rolls and butter, and either eggs or a dish of meat, sausage or fish. Their fifteen-cent dinner consists of a choice of soups, a meat dish, giving a choice of four or five varieties, two kinds of vegetables, dessert, tea, coffee or milk, bread and butter. The same meal in a Bowery restaurant would cost from thirty to fifty cents.

The Squirrel Inn, established by a temperance society to counteract the influence of saloons, was formerly an ordinary Bowery restaurant having a free reading room on the upper floor. On the Bowery it was supposed to be a well-paying restaurant, competing with other restaurants in the neighborhood, apparently a money-making philanthropy. The reading room has been moved to the ground floor and the upper floor is rented out. The same Society maintains the lunch wagons found in various parts of the city. They do nothing towards keeping men out of saloons; the meals they furnish are insufficient in quantity and the prices are relatively higher than in other restaurants. In many of the Bowery restaurants quantity and price are alone considered by the patrons. In these there are plain pinewood tables occasionally polished, kitchen chairs occasionally cleaned, the floors are sanded or covered with sawdust and about the walls are signs giving the price of various dishes and the admonition, "Look out for overcoats and hats." So carefully is this warning observed that patrons rarely remove their overcoats and hats.

There are no table cloths or napkins, the patron's coat sleeve serving the place of the latter; the chinaware is the coarsest and thickest obtainable, forks and spoons are of tin, knives of iron. There are no butter or fish knives, the knife which the diner has just used for fish being next used for butter and a moment later for a meat ball or an apple dumpling.

There are no menus. The bill of fare is posted on a blackboard at the door, or marked with wet chalk upon the window panes, so that the diner can make his selection before entering. The diner gives his order to the waiter, who translates it into the expressive slang of the Bowery as he shouts into the kitchen, "sinkers" for butter cakes, "mystery" for hash, "sleeve-buttons" or two "sunny side up" for two fried eggs, "two shipwrecked" for two fried eggs turned over, "soaked bums" for beets, etc.

The prices in one of the largest of these cheap restaurants are; Coffee, two cents; coffee, bread and butter, five cents; soup, ten cents, but if ordered with meat, five cents; most meat dishes, eight to ten cents; porterhouse steak, fifteen cents; fowl, ten to fifteen cents; vegetables, five cents; dessert, pudding, etc., five cents.

In a still cheaper restaurant on the Bowery soup and meat costs five cents; coffee, bread and butter, and either two eggs or some cereal, five cents. A whole meal, consisting of soup, meat, vegetables, a piece of pie and a cup of coffee, costs ten cents.

The cheapest place charges one cent for soup and bread, two cents for meat and five cents for a meal consisting of soup, meat, a potato, coffee and bread.

Nothing goes to waste in the cheap restaurants. Eggs which may have been returned half a dozen times on account of their odor are sent out again when the next order for eggs comes in, and if finally left over they are used to increase the stuff which goes into next day's hash or "mystery." The various kinds of steak differ only in the size of the portions sent out; veal is used when lamb is ordered and every bit of food brought back is made to do service in another form.

In the five-cent restaurants the bill of fare is exceedingly limited, there being but one kind of soup each day, three meat dishes, steak, hash and stew; one variety of vegetable, potatoes; one kind of dessert, mince pie; two cereals, oatmeal and hominy; besides coffee, tea, milk, bread, butter and eggs. Early comers receive soup, later ones receive soup diluted with water; when the stock is nearly exhausted, diners receive water diluted with soup. The meat is the poorest obtainable and first does service in the soup. What is left over one day goes into the next day's hash or stew.

The meals furnished at the saloon lunch counters, where a small charge is made, are plain and well cooked. The charge is about the same as in ordinary restaurants. Sometimes a simple lunch is prepared for the noon hour and a small charge, five or ten cents, is made for the same. The dives and Raines Law hotels of the brothel class serve no lunch.

The free lunches differ with the class of saloon. Elaborate saloons have usually elaborate free lunches. If a charge is made for lunch during the lunch hour, everything but bread is removed from the free lunch counter during that hour. One saloon, well known for the quantity and variety of its free lunches, supplies the purchaser of a glass of beer with a full meal, consisting of soup, stew, hot sausages, steamed clams or clam chowder, various kinds of meat, sausage and cheese sandwiches, pickles, onions, olives, radishes, etc.

In one saloon, where the size of the glasses is the main attraction, there are three firkins, one filled with pieces of bread, one with beef, cooked meat and sausage, and one with pieces of cheese.

The receptacles are not replenished until empty. Patrons take what they want by the handful and when the bartender is not looking they fill their pockets with the food.

In one saloon each patron receives a roast beef sandwich, the meat being roasted on a spit near the bar.

Of the restaurants supported by philanthropic societies, that attached to the Bowery Branch of the Y. M. C. A. is the best known. A meal consisting of soup, meat or chowder, and coffee and bread costs five cents, but many penniless men receive the meals free. A fair dinner is furnished for fifteen cents.

The lunch wagons, and the restaurants connected with Salvation Army hotels, charge full price for their meals and it is not generally known that they are conducted by philanthropic organizations seeking voluntary contributions. Another restaurant of the same kind, formerly run by the owner of a great sectarian weekly, is one of the poorest, yet probably one of the best paying on the street.

The free meals furnished by missions do more to encourage hypocrisy than evangelical work. Many of the "reformed" wretches who give their testimony and experience do so for the promised meal. Afterwards they go out for more experience. On the night that free lunch is announced the mission is crowded to the doors. Thursday is free lunch night at the Bowery Mission and though the room be half empty on other nights of the week, there is a full house on lunch night.

The only requisite to obtain a meal is that the recipient remains throughout the service. The meal consists of hot coffee, bread and sandwiches. A bread line is formed nightly in front of this mission, where bread is given to every applicant.

Meals are also occasionally distributed at the services of the Volunteers of America.

It is probable that more meals are given away daily by the men who have charge of the free lunch counters in the saloons than by philanthropic organizations in a month.

There is, however, one unostentatious charity which has never appealed for contributions, yet has for years distributed its benefits to all applicants without question.

This is the midnight distribution of bread at Fleischman's bakery, corner Broadway and 11th Street.

At Fleischman's a bread line is formed at midnight at the side door on 11th Street, and as each applicant passes the door a loaf of bread is handed to him. A woman applying for an extra loaf for her family receives it. No questions are ever asked.

While undoubtedly many persons receive a loaf who ought to work or could pay for the same, there are some deserving persons in the line who would rather starve than submit to a humiliating inquisition. During the winter months there are sometimes hundreds in the line.

PART II

THE WRETCHES

THE WRETCHES

CHAPTER I

PARIAHS.

WHO are the wretches of Povertyville? Not the poor who, however unfortunate their lot may be, have conscience as a guiding star and hope as a companion, who have no fear that the morrow may find them in a prison cell, or that their past will bar the gates of salvation to them.

The wretches are those in whom hope is crushed, in whom the still voice of conscience is dumb, in whom avarice and hunger are the moral mentors and in whom the will is at the mercy of the passions.

They are not all indigenous to the soil of Povertyville.

Some are exotics dropping suddenly from the heights of upper-tendom into its whirlpool. Some have drifted from giddy whirls in high social life, gradually descending through successive stages until they reach the lowest

BOWERY TYPES AND CHARACTERS FROM LIFE.

level. Occasionally one goes to Povertyville as one would go to London or Paris. Its life has some rare fascination for him. He goes again and again until he becomes accustomed to its life.

In the words of Pope:

> "Vice is a monster of so hideous a mien,
> As to be hated if but to be seen.
> But seen too often, familiar with its face,
> We first endure, then pity, then embrace."

Here and there one is found who has plunged into the whirlpool of Povertyville to escape some frightful phantom, the shadow of a lost love or a stricken conscience, or to seek forgetfulness from sorrow for a departed loved one or a misspent fortune.

The exotics are easily recognized, for even when near the vortex, where they go down forever, some mark of refinement will present itself.

It may be a mark of neatness such as clean hands, a brushed hat, fringes removed from frayed trousers, or it may be a word or two interspersed in the jargon of the street, better fitted to the drawing room or the lecture hall, or it may be the call for a fashionable drink—a mint julep or absinthe. They never refer to their past. Even those who plunge into the whirlpool to hide their identity from the world and from themselves cannot completely hide every trace of their true selves, for no effort of the will can overcome their repugnance for filth and indecency.

They have a saying, "What's bred in the bone won't come out in the wash," which they apply to themselves. Sooner or later they drift into places where others of their class congregate and where they can be found if wanted. They betray themselves.

The female wretches who show by their manner and speech that they were accustomed to refined surroundings reach Povertyville through many gradations and degradations. Rarely does one drop from a high to a low station in fast life, rarer still is it to find one coming from upper-tendom to Povertyville and there begin her downward course.

Unlike the men, the women do not remain in the places which knew them in their days of innocence.

There are some who are as familiar with Brighton, Aix la Bains and Cannes as with Bar Harbor and St. Augustine, and as familiar with these places as with the New York Tenderloin and the Bowery.

What led these exotics into the currents which end in the vortex of Povertyville's whirlpool?

It is easy to surmise but difficult to prove that misplaced confidence in a lover's vows first led them from the path of rectitude. Some come to escape a harsh father or husband, others began in pique and continued in remorse.

A harsh word or an unjust suspicion drove some from their homes. Some, attracted by the glamor of the footlights, found the tempter at the stage door, while others

THE WRETCHES

began by worshipping a stage idol, forgetting that stage idols have the human passions of other men. A few were born wretches, wretched beings whose earliest recollections are the walls of a foundling asylum, or a wretch for a mother.

The exotics from upper-tendom form but a small proportion of the wretches of Povertyville. Some come from rural districts, most are indigenous.

Thousands of country lads, tired of the dull monotony of farm life, come to the city to emulate the few who have had a successful career. When they fail and reach the end of their resources, they drift into Povertyville.

Here they soon become full-fledged wretches, for they are apt pupils and the ways of vice are not hard to learn. Begging is easy and involves little risk, but the spirit of the young fellow fresh from the country revolts at robbery. Drinking and gambling are later accomplishments.

After one has acquired these vices, if he is still young and strong, he will "cut out" the lover of a woman of the street, either in a fight or while the other is in jail. Then he is in clover. But his fate is like the fate of all such lovers, either a thief ending his days in prison, or a sot who finally reaches the morgue.

With but few exceptions the female wretches from the country belong to one of two classes—stage-struck lasses finally stranded in New York, or pitiable girls deserted by their false lovers, who come to New York for relief and to hide their shame.

The low burlesque companies are responsible for most of the former class.

The girls are attracted by the glitter and glamor of the stage and they want to become actresses. They will work without salary if the manager will give them a chance.

On such terms they are accepted, and the freckled-faced, red-armed, angular farmhand of yesterday now dons the padded fleshings, uses grease paint and stands statuesque in the rear row of the chorus.

The first night away is crucial. The novelty, the glorious prospects, the companions' consolation and the stage-door masher's wine, or the dull, prosaic home and hoe. The wine is the deciding factor. If there be no masher on hand to supply the wine, the manager or some member of the company will supply beer or liquor.

The effect is the same—the morrow brings regrets, but the prospects overcome repentance. After a few seasons, during which she has become world-wise, her sensibilities and sentiment are destroyed, her charms and usefulness on the burlesque stage are gone, she is accustomed to the association of men and to the taste of liquor, and now finds refuge in the Bowery concert halls.

The poor, deluded and deserted victims of man's passions hide their shame and drown their sorrow in the same whirlpool. But they have the same desire for self-preservation as their more fortunate sisters. They sell their body and soul to men, cursing them who buy their favors.

Many of them become opium fiends and find in the fumes of the drug a happy consolation in which perdition is hidden.

The indigenous wretches form classes distinct from the exotics. To many, accustomed from childhood to the all-pervading air of vice, the elevating influence of law and order is lost, these acting merely as a restraint to their passions.

A wretch of this kind is a savage, cowed by fear of the policeman's club, an anarchist in principle, though rejecting the name, often a degenerate with animal instincts more highly developed than those intuitive restraints which we call conscience, sentiment, modesty and honor. A prominent characteristic in this class is aversion to continuous labor and routine. They cannot submit to a superior.

The fear of physical pain and the forcible deprivation of his pleasures and exercise of his passions are the influences affecting him. The policeman is the embodiment of law and his mortal enemy. He knows woman from childhood and her charms and favors from the earliest possible age.

He will work hard if he must, but it is easier to steal, still easier to beg. Devoid of sentiment, he has no friends, but his gregarious nature demands companions, yet for his own safety he will sacrifice his brother. His daring, applied to an honorable calling, would be courage, but there is no chivalry in his nature. Prison conveys no sense of degradation to him; it means to him only compulsory labor and deprivation of pleasure. He is an inveterate gambler, finding less pleasure in his winnings than in the humiliation of a defeated opponent. He will take every unfair advantage over his adversary, as ready to cheat a child out of a penny as a man out of his last dollar. He finds a ferocious delight in the injury he inflicts upon another.

He is an excellent lover to his female companion, and will run any risk to defend her, providing she earns enough to supply his wants; at the same time he is the harshest of tyrants over her. There is no sentiment in such companionship. To him she is a source of income and a means of gratifying his passions without expense; to her he is a paid protector and aid. When she becomes unprofitable he drops her without the slightest scruple or explanation. If he is arrested or loses in a fight with a rival she sheds no tears; he is "down and out" as far as she is concerned. This type of wretch invariably lands in jail. He may have begun his criminal career during childhood, following the example set before him by vicious parents; or he may have begun as a youth, joining one of the gangs of corner loafers who have no visible means of support, yet dress well and spend money, or he may have begun his vicious career as a young man, visiting the dives and attaching himself to one of the women he finds there; all follow the same course which finally lands them in prison. Crime begets crime and the association with criminals leaves its taint. The fellow without conscience, thrown in contact with the more desperate criminals in prison, comes out worse than before. He becomes the ally of the robber and burglar who look for higher game and leaves the Bowery to the petty thief and pickpocket.

Not all the wretches who spring from Povertyville begin as such. Some have heart and conscience and fight like heroes to keep out of its whirlpool. They look beyond their surroundings and make mighty efforts to reach a higher plane. They fail, lose hope, then plunge in madly, caring little how soon the end is reached.

Occasionally one is found who had reached a higher plane. But he had looked back and had seen a woman's smile or heard a tempter's call; or, unaccustomed to prosperity, he had gone through the pittance which was to him wealth, and was back again in Povertyville. Many may be found who until the death of a loving wife or child led righteous lives. Drink brought forgetfulness from sorrow, but it also dulled the mind and conscience and they became sots.

The exotics pass through Povertyville either as homeless, penniless unfortunates, or as drunkards, the former going from penury to beggary, from beggary to vice and crime, the latter becoming sots. The indigenous wretches usually start out as criminals, but those who try to drown sorrow in drink do not follow a criminal career.

And the women who begin their wretched careers in Povertyville? Some are pitiful indeed, well worth sympathy and aid; others have not a redeeming virtue.

Here is the young girl who, like her fallen sister from the country, loved not wisely but too well. Driven to the street by her parents, she goes to a home for fallen women.

Whether it be the home of a wretch or a place for reformation, she receives shelter and learns the ways and wiles of the women of her class. A few months later there is another waif in the foundling asylum and another woman on the street.

There is the young woman whose scanty wages at the machine or behind the counter barely sufficed to keep her body and soul together. Then came the "gentleman friend" who loaned her a few dollars, and then the struggle between gratitude and honor. Gratitude won, her honor lost, the debt was cancelled. 'Tis but a step from granting favors in gratitude for money loaned never to be repaid and granting such favors for the price.

There is the poor wretch who, out of work, out of resources, without friends, without home, goes deliberately "on the town." She seeks aid and advice from some wretch on the street. Wretches though they be, they take the newcomer into their midst and initiate her into the tricks of their trade.

THE WRETCHES

There are many married women on the street. There is the one who, forgetful of her wedding vows, is turned adrift by her husband, then forsaken by her paramour. In despair she goes on the street.

Some have taken up this life on finding that their husbands were unfaithful to them, others are driven to their calling by worthless husbands who live by the shame of the women they had sworn to love, honor and protect.

There are apparently respectable women who solicit on the street while their husbands are at work. They do this to earn pin money and their husbands, unconscious of the source of the money, compliment them for their economy.

Most pitiful is the poor deserted or widowed mother who must ply this trade to furnish food for her little ones. She does not drink, will not steal and is economical, but is a wretch withal.

Then there is the pitiful spectacle—the daughter of a wretch, perhaps a child of dishonor, brought up to follow her mother's vocation. Mother and daughter at the same table, each bidding against the other for the patronage of the same man!

The daughter has seen this life from childhood and has been prepared for it for years. She has no conception of modesty, morality or honor as virtues, but knows how far the law will allow her to go. Her ideas of propriety are determined not by conscience but by statute.

We can account for her lack of rectitude, but how explain the mother's moral obliquity?

Some plunge into the whirl, knowing yet disregarding its dangers. In the giddy whirl they can lead a giddy life, cost what it may. A short life but a merry one is their motto. They are not naturally vicious, but they want pleasure. They lead apparently respectable lives, work by day, but under cover of darkness they hover about or cross the portals which lead to the Underworld of Povertyville.

Once discovered, they throw off all reserve and become the most brazen of wretches. They know right from wrong and will do right as long as it does not interfere with their pleasures and comfort. They become the consorts of criminals and many become opium fiends.

This class is recruited from the working girls who spend their evenings at the dance halls.

There is one class of wretches who, like their male counterparts, are naturally vicious, devoid of moral instincts and conscience. These wretches are not driven to their calling through want, nor take it up for pleasure or in pique; neither do they seek oblivion or death.

Their condition is the result of environment, **perhaps** heredity, and lack of moral teachings. **They seek the** gratification of their passions, the **acquirement of adornments** and freedom from physical exertion.

With savage instincts not repressed by **any inherent** sense of propriety, their actions are governed by their slender knowledge of what the law demands and prohibits. To them virtue and vice are not even relative terms, for without the moral sense to distinguish right from wrong, their conception of these is based upon their likes and dislikes. Fear of punishment has a deterrent effect upon them, but moral and religious teachings are wasted after they once set out upon their vicious career. They become in time the vilest of wretches, vicious and criminal, and are the usual consorts of criminals.

There is still one class of wretches, male and female, we hardly dare mention lest we tread upon forbidden ground. This class is composed of those whose propensities, viler than animal since they have no counterpart in the animal kingdom, place them outside of any human category. They call themselves "fairies." Such a wretch, born of human parents, in the semblance of man gives himself a female appelative, imitates woman's voice and ways, and as far as he dares wears woman's attire.

He plucks out the hair which might form the mustache or beard, uses rouges, powders and cosmetics and all the artifices a woman might use to enhance her charms. Corsets, high-heeled shoes and bracelets are generally worn and in his room he dons complete female attire. This effeminate creature is in love with an equally despicable wretch of his own sex.

There are women of the same class, masculine women who imitate the opposite sex as far as possible. They wear their hair short, shave, employ measures to give their bodies a masculine form and often appear in masculine attire. They assume a gruff voice, and in time lose their natural tone of voice, associate with the "fairies" and in their social intercourse with the latter take the part of a man in his relations to a woman.

They patronize resorts like the Palm, which has been described, and there give exhibitions of their bestial practices under the name of circus performances. They never transfer their affections to the opposite sex. Medical works on sexual perversion deal with this class.

Out of 8,000 professional beggars in this city, not one-fourth are really poor, not one per cent are really deserving. Few beggars ply their trade in Povertyville, and these are, with rare exceptions, lodging-house inmates trying to raise their "hote" money or room rent. These fellows are really poor but not deserving. The professional beggars, the begging letter writers, the "fake bandagers," and the regular "pan-handlers" find the Povertyville district a barren field.

The "fake bandagers," who pose as cripples, go to the shopping district, where they work upon the sympathies of the women, while the regular pan-handlers or beggars who make a living by street begging go to the wealthier districts.

THE WRETCHES

The Bowery beggars ply their trade not to make a living thereby, but to obtain enough to get a drink or two and to get a night's lodging. They are really amateurs, but some are remarkably successful in inventing pleas and raising funds. When they find that they can earn a fair income by begging they graduate into the professional class and desert Povertyville.

CHAPTER II

TEMPTERS AND PARASITES.

THE tempter is worse than the thief.

The opportunity to steal presents itself in innumerable forms and were there none there would still be the opportunity to take by violence what could not be obtained otherwise.

But were there no way to dispose of booty there would be no incentive to steal. Opportunity makes the thief, but the fence is his tempter.

The fence is the man who knowingly buys stolen goods. Formerly when the pawnbroker was not hedged in by restrictions, when the license fee was low and no bond was required, the pawnbroker was the recognized fence. Then, as now, the pawnbrokers were notified by the police of thefts of articles which might be pawned and honest pawnbrokers promptly notified the police when such articles were offered as pledges. But many accepted everything that came along, asked no questions, and if no pawn ticket was asked for, no entry was made. This involved some risk, but a simple and legitimate method of disposing of such property was to make the necessary entry of the article pledged, then, through an

THE WRETCHES

employe, purchase the ticket from the pledger. The employe redeemed the pledge, the proper entry of its redemption was made and all trace of the article was lost.

To-day the pawnbroker is hedged in by many restrictive laws, even a technical evasion of which would involve the loss of his five hundred dollar license. Yet a dishonest pawnbroker will take the risk of accepting a doubtful pledge, advising the pledger to sell the ticket to a dealer in pawn tickets. There are several of these dealers on and near the Bowery. The purchaser of the pawn ticket redeems the pledge and it passes out of his hands at once.

The professional thief, however, does not go to the pawnbroker. He has business relations with a professional fence, who will give him more for the "stuff" than the pawnbroker, who will not betray him, and who will dispose of the goods or make them unrecognizable in a few hours.

The fence is a man of many attainments. He must be an expert jeweler and a passable tailor. He must be able to judge works of art and know how to alter them without seriously impairing their value. His knowledge of the value of all kinds of portable goods must be as extensive as a pawnbroker's. He must have business relations with reputable houses to whom he can refer in an emergency. He must have such relations with dealers who ask no questions, with small manufacturers who will work up goods quickly, and with out-of-town fences to whom goods can be sent when it is necessary to dispose of them elsewhere.

In his relations with the "guns" or thieves, they are strangers to him except at the moment of doing business. If their stuff consists of jewelry or "sparklers" (gems) he is deferential and offers a fair price. If other stuff is brought he drives a hard bargain, and he will never give more than a few cents for each dollar of value. On gold he will give about half of the bullion value. An elaborately-chased watch case has no more value than a plain wedding ring containing the same amount of gold. The usual prices for watch works are, twenty-five cents for American works, fifty cents for Swiss works, and from one to five dollars for a Jurgensen, Howard or expensive American stop watch. On plain silver he gives from twelve to fifteen cents an ounce. There are no general prices for gems. The fence is a shrewd judge of them, and, knowing the source from which they come, he will threaten the novice and try to deceive the experienced. When he can do neither he will offer about as much as the pawnbroker would, or possibly a little more —from one-fourth to one-third of actual value. He will give very little for oddities or rarities, as there is greater risk in disposing of them.

After the fence has received a watch or "super," as the thief calls it, he removes the works from the case and changes the case number by means of a punch. If there are other distinguishing marks on the case these are removed. If they cannot be entirely removed, or too much metal is lost thereby, the case goes into a crucible and in a few minutes it is converted into a lump of gold. If the works are valuable, the number on the train-bridge is altered by means of a punch, then they are replaced in another case. If it is an ordinary American watch, Elgin or Waltham, the train-bridge is unscrewed and another one of the same make taken from a cheap watch is substituted. If it is a very cheap watch the fence simply takes out the works, cleans them and places them in another cheap case. Within a few hours the watch works, whether a hundred dollar Howard or a hundred cent Ingersoll, are ticking away in a new case, probably in the window of a second-hand jewelry store.

When the fence receives pins, rings, earrings, or lockets containing gems, the latter are removed and replaced by others. Engraved jewelry always goes into the melting pot, as these marks cannot be cut out without too much loss. Odd shapes and antiques are hidden a few days for a reward. If none is offered they are altered, or they go into the crucible. Oddities of exceptional value may be hidden for weeks before being altered or reset. They are generally sent out of the city.

Such works of art as paintings, statuettes, etc., which cannot be altered without destroying their value, may be hidden for years, always awaiting a reward. They are finally disposed of in another city, generally to adorn a disreputable house. The fence will never decorate his own house with them. A professional thief will rarely take such articles, however valuable they may be, if anything which can be more easily disposed of is at hand. The fence is an expert tailor and knows how to alter clothing and dresses so as to deceive the rightful owner.

He first removes identification marks, name bands and pocket tags, dyes men's clothing and such woman's apparel as can stand dyeing, then alters the clothing so that they will not fit the owner. Identification is then impossible. The stuff goes to a dealer in second-hand clothing. The fence will not take underwear unless silk, and he will not take cheap goods unless new and in quantity. He will give very little for bulky articles which cannot be readily disposed of or hidden. Rolls of cloth, bundles of clothing and similar goods are sent to a fence who can quickly dispose of such goods. One fence receives nothing but goods in rolls or original packages and he sells them to small shops, where they are worked up into finished material without delay.

One assayer, who has been in business near the Bowery for years, will buy anything which can be converted into bullion. He asks no questions, offers about half of bullion value, and as soon as the deal is concluded the article goes into the melting pot. If a watch is offered the would-be seller must remove the works before the assayer will bid on the case.

So, also, with a diamond-studded locket, or a ring containing a stone. The gem must be removed first before any deal can be made. Filigree, repoussé, chasing or engraving have no value, as the bullion weight alone is considered. Thieves realize more here on plain gold and silver than at the regular fence.

Dealers in second-hand clothing, jewelry and junk sometimes purchase stolen goods knowingly, yet keep within the law. They must not buy from a minor, an apprentice or one whom they know to be a servant. They must not buy between sunset and 7 A. M. and they must enter in a book a description of the article, the time of the purchase and the name and address of the seller.

If anything they purchase answers to the description of an article advertised as lost or stolen, they must notify the police.

These are the principal regulations governing their business. They are permitted to sell an article as soon as they purchase it, and this always happens when they purchase doubtful goods. They need make no entry of the sale and it is impossible to trace an article after it leaves their hands. Professional thieves do not patronize second-hand clothing or jewelry dealers, as the dealers will betray them to save the license on which their business depends.

The only stuff that the thief must dispose of directly to the dealer is junk. It is safe to assume that half the lead pipe, door knobs, window weights, copper kettles, etc., received by the small junk dealers, are the proceeds of thefts too insignificant to be reported to the police. They are, therefore, comparatively free from interference in their business.

The most serious feature of this is that junk stealing is too small and unprofitable to be taken up by men, and boys are easily encouraged to take lead pipe, brass door knobs, and other metals from vacant houses and their own homes, to be sold to the junk dealers for a few cents.

While much stolen property sooner or later finds its way into second-hand jewelry stores and pawnbrokers' sales stores, the dealers do not purchase such articles from the thieves. The fence is the go-between. The receivers of the stolen property are the prime tempters of the thieves.

The parasites, those who grow rich from the proceeds of the booty and vice, are the gambling-house keepers, the dive keepers, Raines Law hotel keepers, the "madams" who run "ladies' boarding houses," and the wretches who sell their favors on their own account.

The criminals spend their money chiefly in gambling houses and upon their female companions. "Easy come, easy go."

Some of the gambling houses are run by ex-convicts who have retired from more hazardous occupations after having made a rich haul. Those in Povertyville are run in the name of a club, or by a sporting character.

THE WRETCHES 119

Rumor says they are controlled by a member of a well-known family of East Side politicians, but it is impossible to prove this connection. Hearsay is not legal proof.

The managers of the gambling houses are ordinary small sports who pose as owners in an emergency.

During a reform administration, and when they are under police surveillance, the gambling house is run as a club and none are admitted who are not known by the manager or vouched for by a reliable habitue. At such a time the game is honestly conducted, as the frequenters are without exception skilled gamblers. When the town is run open and there is no police interference, strangers are admitted and marked cards, loaded dice, crooked faro boxes and roulettes, sleight-of-hand tricks in shuffling and dealing—all are used to enrich the gambler and cheat the novice.

Most dive keepers start out as waiters or bartenders.

A few began in ordinary saloons; most, however, were first waiters in dives, then head waiters, and afterwards managers. A few dive keepers began by opening saloons on or near the Bowery with the firm intention to keep their places clean and orderly.

It is impossible to conduct a new saloon profitably on the Bowery on bar patronage alone, unless some special inducement is offered. Even an extra large glass or a free lunch no longer attracts. When the saloon keeper finds that he cannot run a respectable saloon profitably while his neighbors make money through well-patronized back rooms, he will either follow suit or go out of business.

If he has a reputation to uphold, he may give the place a fanciful name, secure a new license under an assumed name, or in the name of his manager, partition off the rear part of the saloon, put in a number of chairs and tables, and the place is now a dive.

The owner of one such place, recently closed, opened it is a clean, orderly saloon. By discouraging toughs and disreputable characters his place became known as a respectable saloon with a good class of patrons. But there was not enough of this to make the place pay, and he was on the verge of bankruptcy. The place was closed, and opened a few days later under a new management. It received a distinctive title, a new license was secured under an assumed name, a large back room was formed by a partition placed at the end of the bar, and a manager was hired. This manager was a well-known dive keeper and his reputation soon brought all the wretches of Povertyville to the place. Many of the latter had known the manager in his earlier days in the Tenderloin. The place prospered, the real owner opened a good hotel in a nearby seaside resort, under his own name, and he is there a respected citizen. A brewing company aided him in the conversion of his saloon into a dive.

A few dive keepers are boxers or otherwise connected with sporting affairs. Their resorts are usually opened and owned by a brewer, who pays the manager a salary and commission on sales, for the use of his name and services. These consist in standing before or behind the bar, drinking with any one who wants to treat, and assuming the responsibility of ownership. He rarely visits the back room, but turns the management of that part of the business over to the head waiter. Sporting men are notorious spendthrifts, and the reputed owners or keepers of these dives are no exceptions to the rule. They are discriminating in their charities, however, and never aid the panders and other wretches who enrich them. The unfortunate fellow who does not drink, the broken-down, old-time sport, and the Salvation Army lassie never go away empty-handed.

Far different is the dive keeper who rose from the ranks of waiters and bartenders.

He is heartless and conscienceless, trusts none and is trusted by none, his every action being governed by the question of what will the immediate profit be? He does not figure upon future returns, as he is well aware that the police lightning might strike him at any moment.

He is usually found seated near the door of his back room, where he can overlook the place and from which he can make a hasty exit when necessary.

Strangers, unless partly intoxicated, are distrusted and made uncomfortable by waiters and bouncers. A visitor seen taking notes is unceremoniously thrown out.

The stranger who is intoxicated is conducted to a table where several women are seated. While he spends his money for drinks he is not molested, but when his money is gone, he is carried or thrown out. If he appears to have valuables about him, one of the women sits on his lap, engages him in lewd conversation, at the same time removing the contents of his pockets, the booty being passed to her lover behind her. The dive keeper receives a share of this later.

One well-known dive keeper to whose place reference has been made, would permit no robbery in his dive. This man was the most notorious of his class, yet there was nothing in his personality, manners, dress or speech which would lead one to suspect his vocation.

Outside of his resort he could pass as a retired merchant. While he could be as foul as the foulest of his customers, with gentlemanly strangers he was courteous, quiet, never coarse or vulgar. They say he has retired from business, but those who say they know, claim he still owns two Bowery resorts, one a Raines Law hotel run by his son, another a sporting resort, run by his former bouncer, a well-known pugilist.

Among the Raines Law hotel owners there are many respectable saloon keepers who have been forced to employ the hotel subterfuge in order to sell beer and liquor on Sunday. At the same time this law furnishes a loophole whereby disreputable resorts are legalized, and as the New York district attorney stated before the State

THE WRETCHES 123

legislature in February, 1903, out of the 2,500 places licensed in the city under that law, less than 200 were honest and respectable hotels. The "Committee of Fourteen," organized to wipe out the vicious resorts opened under this law, has reduced the number of Raines Law hotels to 800.

This vicious makeshift of a law has done away with the furnished room houses where rooms could be hired by couples by the hour. Such houses were found in a few localities where the women congregated. There was nothing to indicate their character to passersby, and there was no such notoriety attached to them as is now attached to even the respectable Raines Law hotel.

This law, since amended, has scattered nearly 1,000 such houses all over the city; it has made a saloon a necessary adjunct to them; it has given the saloon keeper who could stand the necessary expense a means to violate the spirit of the excise laws, and it has given the character of the Raines Law hotel a publicity and a notoriety which is a disgrace to the city.

An unfortunate feature in connection with this law is, it has produced a moral turpitude or degeneration in hundreds of saloon-keepers who formerly abhorred the bare idea of harboring a dissolute person.

After the Raines Law was passed these men found that they could not conduct their business profitably without adding the ten rooms necessary to procure a hotel license. Then, to make the hotel profitable, they were obliged to admit these wretches.

Those Raines Law hotels which were opened to take the place of the furnished room houses are conducted by dive keepers or managed by men accustomed to handle dive habitues.

Far more profitable than either the furnished room house or the Raines Law hotel is the ordinary brothel, or "Ladies' Boarding House," as the cards of one of them announce.

These are usually conducted by a woman who was economical while on the street and has an energetic lover, or "husband."

A description of "Mrs. Schneider," who conducted a resort of this kind for years near the Bowery, will illustrate the general characteristics of these wretches.

This woman had been on the street for a few years, was careful of her health, drank little, and was saving.

At first she had a furnished room, and by an arrangement with the housekeeper, her patrons were obliged to hire the room whenever they accompanied her to it. Later she kept a furnishd room house, which she soon converted into a ladies' boarding house. A burly fellow, picked up in a dive, posed as Mr. Schneider, her protector, bouncer and man of all work. Material for her establishment was plentiful. In the beginning she took city and country girls who were cast adrift by false lovers, helped them out of their difficulties and gave them a home. When the supply of these no longer met the demands of her patrons, procuresses sent girls to her from abroad. She took excellent care of the wretches in her house, for upon their health and beauty depended her livelihood. She knew what would make a lean girl plump and what would reduce the obese, and regulated their diet accordingly. A physician called weekly and certified to their freedom from disease. When one became too ill to receive visitors, she could not receive another morsel of food until she had recovered. The girl was then taken to the door of the hospital and left there.

The girls in the house were forcibly detained, being deprived of their clothes, except a low-necked, short-skirted Mother Hubbard gown, the usual reception dress. When a girl became obstreperous she was starved into submission.

Mrs. Schneider charged the girls for board and medical services, and allowed them a small part of their earnings from visitors, so little, however, that a girl seldom got out of debt. When a girl became "old stock" she was turned out of the house, or, if still attractive, she was traded or sold to another establishment.

The girls rarely gave trouble, as they led an indolent, quiet life, free from care, thoughtless of the future.

Mrs. Schneider was a shrewd judge of human nature, could be refined or vulgar as would best suit her patrons, fearless, without conscience or heart, and without womanly instincts. She paid liberally for protection, owed nobody (in fact, nobody trusted her), and her every act was governed by mercenary motives.

She became wealthy and, after her place was raided, she was arrested, forfeited her bail, and left her girls in the hands of the police. She was typical of her class.

Women running establishments which are liable to be closed at any moment rent the house and furniture and invest their money in jewelry which can be readily converted into cash. They are always ready for flight, and when such a course is necessary they leave little of value behind.

Besides the regular source of income from the girls, a considerable profit is derived from the sale of liquors without a license, but a more profitable source of income is the rental of girls for special occasions. A person known to the madam can hire a girl for a day or a night as companion at a social affair. The charge for the girl is generally five dollars a day, and from one to fifty dollars for the clothing and jewelry she is to wear.

The procuress is usually an old "madam" who is familiar with the girls kept in the different establishments and in foreign resorts. There was until recently in a suburb of Hamburg an exchange for girls intended for brothels. Here the procuress would go annually and pick out her stock. Just as in the slave trade of antebellum days, so the girls were obliged to pass muster, the trader in women's flesh and virtue examining the girls as the old slavers did the slaves. Face, form, texture, mentality, all were examined and, if found satisfactory, the girls came to New York as daughters or servants of the procuress. The immigration laws are stopping this traffic, but some girls still come in consigned to "aunts," who sell them to brothels.

Male procurers, or "cadets," have taken up this infamous trade during the last five years. They do not look for dissolute women, but try to induce respectable girls to take up shameful lives or inveigle them into disreputable houses. They will not hesitate to marry a girl or use force to carry out their purpose, and one who is now in prison is said to have married six victims, delivering each one afterwards into a brothel. The severe punishment inflicted upon these wretches has had a deterrent effect upon their trade.

CHAPTER III

FACTORS DEVELOPING WRETCHES.

NATIONALITY, race and religion are appreciable factors in directing the trend of the vicious. Vice and crime are not bound by nationality or creed, but some forms of vice and crime are more prevalent in some nationalities and races than in others. Thus, one rarely sees a Jewish beggar, while German beggars are quite common. When counterfeit coin appears in a neighborhood the government officials look through the nearest Italian quarter for the counterfeiters. One rarely sees an Italian beggar or drunkard, and there are few confirmed criminals among them. Their crimes are generally assault in some form, due to passion or revenge. The Americans and the Irish are more daring than others, and they will incur greater risks.

Nearly all the more desperate criminals, those who undertake large jobs, like burglary, belong to one of these two nationalities. Gambling proclivities are most pronounced in the Americans, and they run the gambling houses and pool-rooms. Gambling is also prevalent among Hungarians, who play in the coffee saloons along lower Second Avenue and in the side streets, and among the Italians, who play in saloons in "Little Italy," as the district around and to the north of Mulberry Bend Park is called.

The Jew will not run any risk whereby his life might be endangered. He will, therefore, not undertake the more dangerous work of the house-breaker or thief; neither will he handle the rough customers found in the dives. This work is left to the Irish waiters and bouncers and these become later the dive-keepers. The concert halls, however, are generally conducted by Jews. The fence is generally an American Jew, and to this race belong nearly all those in whose business dickering and trading is possible. There are comparatively few Germans among the wretches, and these have no special vicious trend. While there are many German prostitutes, the men lack the daring necessary to become great or dangerous criminals, neither have they the acumen to become successful competitors in the lines followed by the Jews. We rarely hear of a German burglar or highwayman, and seldom of a German dive-keeper or gambling-house keeper. More often we find German waiters in vicious concert halls; sometimes they keep brothels, some live by craft or fraud, many are beggars.

In considering race and religion as factors in relation to crime and vice we must not forget composite tendencies, hereditary and acquired, in wretches of foreign birth. As an example we find the Jew with his inherent commercial capacity, and the natural characteristics of the land of his birth. To these are added the new tastes, desires, methods, etc., acquired here. With the exception of the commercial instinct which persists, his character is moulded by environment and association, and, being naturally of a plastic disposition, he is led into a virtuous or vicious direction without much difficulty. At the same time, lacking that physical daring which we term bravado, he will not follow in ways where such daring is required. He will not fight and will keep away from occupations in which brawls may be expected. If he is a Hungarian he will probably follow the national trend of gambling, and run a coffee saloon, where gambling is the principal feaure. The Russian Jew will prefer an occupation where trading is possible, preferably the sale of second-hand goods. The German Jew has no prominent national characteristics, and more readily adopts the characteristics of the American. If viciously inclined he will follow any line where his hereditary business instinct can combine with a vicious career. He will run a concert hall, or brothel, or become a fence. In the American Jew the national characteristics predominate over the racial instinct. He possesses more courage than the foreigner, loves to gamble, and lacks to a great extent that religious feeling which acts upon the foreign-born Jew as a restraint to viciousness. If viciously inclined he will become either a crooked sport or a fence. Some who are taught to become sneak thieves and pickpockets when young develop into shoplifters and thieves. The Ameri-

THE WRETCHES 131

cans possess courage, shrewdness, and a speculative instinct, and they follow lines where these characteristics are brought into play. If they take up a vicious career they undertake the more daring crimes, like housebreaking and street robbery, or fraud where craft or finesse are required, or they are gamblers and sports, taking greater risks than any other nationality. The Irish possess the same kind of courage as the Americans, are more tenacious of purpose, are as a rule physically stronger, but lack the shrewdness, or rather the craft, of the Americans, nor is the speculative or gambling instinct greatly developed. They therefore take up those lines where their qualities are most useful, as waiters, bouncers, dive keepers, saloon keepers, keepers of Raines Law hotels, and perpetrators of crimes of violence. We can in the same way trace the influence of race, religion and nationality upon the form of crime and vice throughout all the nationalities which make up the wretches of Povertyville.

We find the same factors at work among the female wretches of Povertyville.

All races and nationalities are found among the women of the street, but great changes have occurred in this respect in the last thirty years. In the seventies a Jewish prostitute was a rarity, now there are many. This is mainly due to economic conditions and to the fact that women are now thrown into more intimate contact with men since they take up occupations which bring this about. Formerly, when procuresses came from Europe weekly with scores of German women for brothels, there were more of this nationality than at present. The number of Irish girls on the street has increased enormously. In the seventies the brothels held mainly German and American girls, with some Irish and a few French girls. Now the Irish and Americans are far in the majority, there are still many Germans, and some Jewish girls, while the French have almost disappeared from Povertyville. In the foreign colonies there are brothels having women of the nationality of the colony, and near the water front there are some having Scandinavian women for the sailors of those countries.

The Irish and the American women associate with the more daring of the men, and many become shoplifters. The German women prefer to keep brothels, while Jewish women, true to their trading instincts, become, in time, procuresses.

Little need be said of other nationalities, as there are few other nationalities except Italians represented among the wretches of Povertyville. The Italians have vices as glaring as the others, but, being clannish, their vices are not on public exhibition. The vicious Italian woman does not walk the streets, but receives her patron in her home. Gambling is carried on in homes and in saloons which are patronized by Italians alone. Other forms of depravity are confined to the home or the saloon, and are not exposed to the stranger. There are few criminals among Italians, the majority of crimes being acts of violence in passion or revenge, and their own country people are usually the victims. The only other crimes with which they are often charged are the manufacture and passing of counterfeit coin, an occupation that the counterfeiters bring with them from Italy. The French have almost entirely disappeared from Povertyville, and there are now no brothels of the kind prevalent in the seventies, when French madams introduced new forms of vice and bestiality in the district. The old French quarter in the neighborhood of Bleecker Street and West Broadway still harbors a few of the wretches of that nationality, but these are rarely seen on the Bowery. When a vicious Frenchman does find his way into the Bowery district it is to become a waiter in a concert hall.

While there is generally some modesty among the female wretches of other nationalities this trait seems to be lacking in the French cocotte. She will give bestial exhibitions which are repulsive to other lewd women, will appear nude without the slightest hesitancy if she receives her price, exhibiting chic and coquetry, but not a trace of modesty. Her charms and abandon secure for her a place in fashionable brothels, and she need not go to Povertyville for admirers. Many work on their own account, and being economical, they save enough in a few years to return to France and there lead a respectable life. These are found in the Tenderloin since French brothels have left Povertyville.

THE WRETCHES

There are many lewd women of the Slavonic race: Hungarians, Bohemians and Russians, among the wretches of Povertyville. Some of them have been brought over for brothel purposes, some were sent here by false lovers, who promised to follow but failed to do so; some were lured over under promise of good paying positions. While there is much immorality among the Slavs, few of the women take up vicious careers after they have been engaged here in honest vocations. Those that do so remain in their national colony, and are rarely found soliciting on the street or in public dives. Most of these foreigners go to brothels and remain there until they have learned the English language, then they go out to dives or are sent to other brothels.

The prevailing vices among the Chinamen are opium smoking and gambling. In sensual vices they do not differ from the whites, but they seem to prefer to consort with white women, and there are many white women in Chinatown who have become opium fiends, and will consort with the Mongolians for a thimbleful of the drug.

The vices of the northern Negro are not due to inherent depravity, but to ignorance and a lower standard of morality. Sensuality and gambling are common vices. Their crimes are mainly petty thefts, rarely associated with violence. The so-called "bad nigger," the one who carries a razor, is simply a bully among his own people, just like the bad white man who carries a pistol is a bully among his class. The southern Negro whose notorious crimes, rape and assault upon white women, are so often summarily punished, does not come north. The indigenous Negro is a different specimen of humanity, has different tastes and traits, and prefers to associate with lewd women of his own race.

Beside race and nationality the factor of occupation plays a part in the trend toward vice and crime, and the conversion of respectable men and women into wretches. The first contact of a person of refinement and decency with the coarse tough or vile woman of the street excites disgust. Thrown constantly in contact with the wretches, especially if one derives his livelihood from them, a man takes a more liberal view of their mode of life, extenuates, excuses and finally justifies and upholds their faults. In some occupations men are constantly exposed to vicious influences, and sooner or later succumb to them. This is especially true of night bartenders and waiters, men in the show business, especially in the small traveling companies; men selling plated jewelry, etc. It is safe to say that nearly every dive keeper in New York was at one time a waiter or bartender in a respectable saloon. From the respectable saloon he goes to a tough saloon or dive, becomes head waiter, manager, and afterwards owner. Or he may have opened a decent saloon, permitted the vicious to congregate there, and these finally drove out the better class of patrons. Bartenders are often asked to take some article of jewelry as a pledge from a patron who has run short of funds. Sometimes the pledge is redeemed; frequently, however, it is the proceeds of a robbery, and the pledger, if he does return, will tell the bartender to dispose of it. In this way the bartender becomes a fence. When the high license and Raines Law went into effect many good saloon keepers found their Sunday trade cut off, and secured hotel licenses. To make the hotel adjunct of ten bedrooms pay, the rooms were let out to couples, and the saloon keeper became a keeper of a Raines Law hotel, or virtually a brothel keeper. Most gambling house managers and keepers began their sporting careers behind the bar of a saloon.

Men in the theatrical business are exposed to temptations from within the company and from without. In the small traveling companies, more particularly in the burlesque companies which carry from six to ten men and from ten to fifteen women, few are married. Traveling together for months, stopping at the same hotels and boarding houses, indiscriminate intercourse is frequent. This lowers their respect for woman's honor. Everywhere on the road the actor receives letters from foolish women who would submit to his desires for the honor of talking to an actor and perhaps getting a free pass, and this further lowers his respect for all women. His principal pastimes are gambling and drinking and entertaining jolly companions. The small fry in the theatrical profession, if they marry at all, select their partners from the professional ranks. The others break down in time through their excesses, many take up opium smoking and some become sports and gamblers. When they reach Povertyville they are either broken-down sports, sots or pipe or cocaine fiends.

Men dealing in imitation jewelry find the wretches of Povertyville good customers. The wretches make money easily and spend it readily for baubles. One may steal a watch worth fifty dollars, sell it to a fence for five dollars and pay the five for a plated watch worth two dollars and believe he has the best of the bargain. Or he may trade the stolen watch for a Rhinestone plated ring worth fifty cents, knowing that the dealer has only imitation jewelry, yet hoping that the dealer has made a mistake. The dealer, finding it so easy to dupe these people, tries the same game with others and later branches out in other lines of fraud. It has been repeatedly charged that the police are in collusion with the criminals and protect them. It is impossible to get together in any vocation a body of 7,000 men without finding some scamps among them; but to charge the body for the faults of a few is certainly a gross injustice to the whole. It is true that some men having political influence follow unlawful occupations without police interference and that police officers who were supposed to devote their whole time and attention to the business of the department have been able to accumulate many times the amount of their salary. The deplorable conditions existing before the Lexow investigation do not prevail to-day, and it is safe to say that the police are not the associates of the wretches, though they may overlook the infraction of excise laws and to some extent the laws against gambling and soliciting.

There are some pursuits in which those who follow them are constantly exposed to temptation. The junk dealer is importuned by boys to buy old brass, copper and lead. After he has made a few such purchases, paying cents for what he will receive dollars in return, and finds that there is little risk in detection, he will induce the boys to bring more stuff and may even tell the boys how to cut lead and pull out brass door knobs. The dealer in old clothing is likewise tempted to purchase stolen wearing apparel. The pawnbroker cannot ask a person who offers a pledge to prove his identity and will take a pledge which he may have reason to suspect has been stolen.

We can also include among those who are exposed and sometimes succumb to temptation, the druggists. They are asked to supply "hop," the opium extract used by smokers, and other morphine and opium preparations, knockout drops, cocaine, appliances and drugs used for immoral purposes. Physicians who make a specialty of criminal operations are withal criminals, while those who examine the inmates of brothels are often asked to help unfortunate girls out of their difficulties and rarely refuse. Some lawyers who make a specialty of criminal cases associate with the criminals and vicious and advise them how to circumvent the law. There is a wide span between the extremes of legal and moral honesty, which some lawyers attempt to bridge by craft instead of conscience.

Among women occupation is a more important factor in the development of wretches than among men. In some lines of work so many fall that a stigma has been cast upon the occupation affecting the good name of all following it. There are hundreds of good, honest, virtuous chorus girls, even among the cheap burlesque companies. Yet chorus girls are exposed to so many temptations in the company and from without, and so many succumb to temptation that more than a shade of suspicion rests upon all. Some withstand every temptation until they find that there is an imputation of doubt in the respectability of chorus girls as a class. Then, falling back upon the saying, "If I have the name I'll have the game," they submit. Some are initiated by other girls of the company, who find delight in destroying the virtue of innocent girls. This is a common trait among vicious women. While the male wretches will not intentionally corrupt men or boys who are good, the female wretches make efforts to drag others down to their level. The innocent chorus girl receives flattering invitations from men, sees with envy the finery and jewelry given to the vicious by admirers, and is taunted by the others for her weakness and cowardice. Some resist the taunts but are flattered by the attentions from admirers and fall. Some in a spirit of bravado, and stung by taunts, accept the first comer; some gradually overcome moral scruples and the fear of physical consequences, associate with the vicious, drink with them and while under the influence of liquor make their first false step.

Waitresses in restaurants are constantly exposed to temptation and many fall. Girls employed in manicure establishments are peculiarly exposed, are continually thrown into immodest contact with men and are obliged to listen to veiled and often open allusions to immoral subjects. In no other occupation followed by women is it so difficult to remain virtuous and modest.

Many chambermaids in hotels, not so much in New York hotels as in hotels in the smaller cities, earn an occasional dollar beside their wages from the male guests. If drummers' tales are true some hotels on the road have pretty chambermaids who can be had by applying to the clerk. Domestics in homes are often exposed to the sensual desires of the male members of the family and often fall. In one home for fallen women 92 out of 162 gave their occupation as domestics.

There are other occupations in which women are exposed to temptation through being thrown into intimate contact with men. The cloak model must submit to the scrutiny of buyers of business houses, and these are not always satisfied with merely looking at the shape and fit of the garment. Artists' models, as a rule, remain chaste. The credit therefor is due as much to the artist as to the model, for while face, form and posture may arouse sensual desires, the artist must suppress these desires if he wants to do good work. With the mind imbued with the spirit of the subject he is working upon, his model is to him merely a part of the necessary implements of his craft. Her personality affects him as little as does the form and beauty of the patient when the physician is making his diagnosis. The models who appear before classes are occasionally sought after by art students in whom the exposure and posture arouse desires, but when the model falls it is generally due to some admirer not in artistic life. Nurses in hospitals are likewise exposed to temptations through their more intimate contact with men, but remain chaste. Devotion to their work and the thought that the men are patients are the influences restraining them, aside from the inherent moral instinct.

When a woman is thrown into constant contact with a man under conditions where they are alone and are not subject to outside interference, if there is anything attractive in either they will be attracted to each other. Such attraction leads to pleasant relations which in time become social and finally intimate. Many girls employed as private secretaries, stenographers and typewriters are placed in such a position that they are alone for hours or days with their employers. If the girl is viciously inclined and seeks to inveigle her employer she soon finds an opportunity to carry out her object. It is generally, however, the man who makes the first advances. A rainy day, when dinner for both must be brought in from a neighboring restaurant, may be followed the next day by an invitation to take dinner together outside of the office. If she accepts she will later be invited to go to the theater. When the girl has gone that far she will show her gratitude by permitting him to go further. The foolish girl accepts her employer's advances because she imagines that he is in love with her and has perhaps read about employers who married their typewriters. The giddy girl wants a good time and is proud to think that her employer will take her out. Some girls submit believing they will lose their positions if they do not favor the employer; others expect an increase in salary. Whatever method the employer may use to make the initial advances, the end is the same—the girl falls, and once down, she will generally remain down unless she has an opportunity to marry.

It would be an injustice to cast a slur upon an occupation which thousands of hard-working women and girls follow. Indeed, as a body, the stenographers and typewriters are in morality above reproach. But we hear too often of the pretty typewriter who goes to lunch with her employer and such intimacy is not conducive to the good repute of the individual or of the class. Where there are hundreds placed in the position we have described and so many fall through the causes stated, we must consider their occupation as a factor in the development of wretches.

Most of the wretches who began their vicious career while employed in shops and factories blame their first misstep to curiosity or jealousy. The favorite topics of conversation among shop girls are dresses, amusements, and "the fellows"—the last principally. The vicious ones make no secrets of their liaisons, excite the good girl's imagination with description of the pleasures, quiet her fears of the physical consequences by telling her tricks that many married women do not know. The girl's curiosity overcomes her conscientious scruples and fears, and the vicious girl supplies the accommodating friend.

This also applies to offices and stores. A foreman or overseer in a factory may have a favorite who will receive special privileges. If she is tardy, careless or lazy he will be lenient with her and harsh to another who objects to the injustice. While some girls will submit to injustice rather than hazard their position or reputation, others will endeavor to gain the foreman's good will, even at the cost of their virtue. Sometimes there is the hope of advancement or fear of discharge, a promise or threat, expressed or implied, to break down a good girl's resolutions. A girl may submit to her lover when her devotion overcomes her conscientious scruples, and under such circumstances she will remain faithful to him. But when a girl submits to an employer it is the beginning of a downward career which usually ends on the streets of Povertyville. Unchastity with a lover often leads to speedy marriage; with an employer or superior it is often followed by indiscriminate immorality and prostitution. While in many occupations employes are peculiarly exposed to temptation and fall, similar conditions may induce opposite thoughts, virtuous or vicious, depending upon accompanying circumstances. The face, form and posture of the chorus girl may arouse admiration with sensual thoughts when on the stage, yet when exhibited before an art class there may be admiration without a trace of sensuality. The intimate contact of the nurse and her patient produces a far different effect upon both from the intimate contact of the manicurist and her male patron. The waiter in a dive becomes debased by his contact with the vicious, while the piano player in the same dive may retain his respectability. A peculiar feature of occupation as a factor in the development of vice, is the large number of fallen women who give their occupation as seamstress, dressmaker or milliner, occupations which do not bring them in contact with men.

Most of these ascribe their fall to the desertion of a lover or husband. Many blame drink, especially after a dance, when, heated by the exertion of dancing and the close ballroom, they were induced to take some liquor, cooling for a moment but intoxicating afterwards. After they had taken two or three of such drinks they became unconscious of the further proceedings.

No mention has been made of poverty or social conditions as a factor in the development of wretches. Cases occur where a hungry man will steal and a hungry woman will go on the street, but unless there is a vicious trait the act is done in desperation and is followed by remorse. These are not wretches. The great mass of the poor are not vicious, but, accustomed to their simple mode of life, they abhor vice and crime. When persons accustomed to luxuries come down in the world quickly, they find that they cannot readily accommodate themselves to poverty. In their efforts to rise, if there be any vicious trait in them it will come out at this time, and such a person is likely to become vicious or criminal. There are black sheep in the families of the rich and poor and no psychological study can account for them. Occasionally we can find a hereditary strain. More often there are vicious environments. Lack of religious teachings has been given as a factor, yet there are few of the wretches who have not had such teachings. Under favorable conditions these act as a restraint to the passions, but, given the opportunity, or let envy, avarice or jealousy be aroused, or hunger be felt, and the restraint is instantly dropped as though it were a cloak. Once dropped, the various factors will develop the vicious trait and determine its trend. In considering these factors we must remember that there are national and racial traits which may be perfectly proper among such nations and races, while if exhibited by others they would be considered immodest, immoral and vicious.

CHAPTER IV

CURIOUS CHARACTERS.

THE underworld of Povertyville hides many curious characters. Not all are criminals nor even vicious; indeed, there are some who apparently have none of its vices, are not criminals, yet associate with criminals, are exposed to their temptations, discuss nefarious plans with them, yet never enter into any dishonest scheme, nor do they betray those whose confidence they have obtained.

Some of evident refinement are not without means, but almost all who are educated and refined are drunkards or drug fiends.

There is old Shakespeare, who will quote an extract from the immortal bard when he asks you for the price of a drink, and, if plied with liquor, he will repeat whole scenes from his plays. Some one has been paying his rent in a Bowery lodging house for the past ten years, and he makes enough by begging in his peculiar way to keep himself supplied with liquor and food.

Another educated wretch is Daddy Ward, boon companion of Shakespeare when both are in their cups, but each avoids the other when he is sober. Daddy is prob-

BOWERY TYPES AND CHARACTERS FROM LIFE.

ably the only one on the street who knows Shakespeare's history. In his sober moments he refers to his friend as the bum, but when both are drunk he will sometimes call him professor. Shakespeare looks like an old ragged tramp, but Daddy wears a frock coat buttoned to the neck, a white collar, tie and cuffs. In his lodging house they say strings take the place of suspenders, his ties are strips from his last white shirt and his only other shirt, the red flannel shirt he is wearing, might be mistaken for a crazy quilt. No one knows how Daddy lives, as he does not beg, yet he has never more than a few cents in his pocket. He occasionally speaks of Ball, Black & Company, Fisk and Hatch, Jay Cooke and Sam Sloan—always execrating the last two.

Parker—"Mr. Parker," if you please, if you should forget to prefix the "Mr."—was an architect, judging from his favorite topic of conversation. Evidently an Englishman, with a broad Yorkshire dialect, he claims to be an American. He says he knows nothing of English churches, but will describe minutely famous continental churches and other architectural features. Some one pays his room rent and gives him a small weekly allowance, which he spends in a Bowery morgue.

"Dutchy," who has been kicked out of every saloon where a lunch counter is near the door, shows on his face the scars inflicted by the German University Schlager, and has at times the bearing of a military officer. He is a keen student of human nature and generally strikes the right plea to rouse the sympathy of a possible donor of the price of a drink. He is overbearing and has been repeatedly kicked, cuffed and beaten, yet he has been known to give his only dime to pay for another unfortunate's bed, then go out and beg for more.

There is Jack, or J. Black, under which name he registers. He is evidently well connected, but hides his identity under a ragged suit, and comports himself like one of the unfortunates. Jack is neat, uses good language and does not drink. He is always provided with funds, but no one knows the source of his income. Occasionally he puts on a good suit and disappears for a few days, but ordinarily he spends his days in the reading room of a library near by. Although he has been in one lodging house for five or six years, the other lodgers know no more about him now than they did when he first arrived.

Scotty is another curious character who seems to have an unfailing source of income. When his funds are low he writes to someone in Scotland, cries as he writes, is morose until he receives an answer, then cries again. He will then disappear for a week or more, but he always turns up in a new suit, drunk and hilarious. He pays his room rent for months in advance.

Tom Curtis, an Englishman, who has apparently no vices, has a habit of disappearing for a month or two, then returns to his lodging house for a few months. When stopping at the lodging house he rarely goes out except for meals, spending his time reading novels and smoking. He is probably well connected, but he has no friend or confidant among his fellow lodgers.

Carey is an old rounder who has been on the street for many years, following a regular cycle. When in funds he goes to one of the more pretentious lodging houses and to good restaurants. As his funds decrease he goes to cheaper places, finally reaching the ten-cent lodging houses and eating at free lunch counters. When his funds are entirely exhausted he will do the menial work in saloons for the privilege of sleeping in a chair or on a cask, and his meals consist of remnants left on the lunch counter. Then he disappears, but in a few days he turns up again at the good lodging house. The whole cycle lasts three months. When he buys clothing his money is soon exhausted and he goes to the cheap lodging house in a few weeks, but this is the only variation in his routine. He has probably a small quarterly income which, if properly applied, would suffice to secure him fair accommodations and meals throughout the quarter.

These wretches or unfortunates carefully conceal their identity and history, but there are some who will introduce themselves to every prospective donor.

One of these, now near the end of his career, was in his day one of the greatest bareback riders in the world. He thought he understood race horses as well as he did circus horses, and his princely salary was left at the race track. Then he became a heavy drinker, lost his nerve after a severe fall from a horse while drunk, and his friends deserted him. Now he begs for the price of a night's lodging.

This wretch has a friend who, like himself, gained fame in the circus ring and is now ending his days as a Bowery sot. While the one roused the admiration of thousands by his daring, the other gained their applause by his whimsicalities and acrobatic misadventures. He was one of the best known circus clowns. Today his son provides for his lodging and meals and makes a weekly allowance for drink. There are several who were once familiar with the applause which is bestowed upon the popular actor.

Here is one hobbling along, a mental and physical wreck. He is unknown to the present generation, but in the days of the blood-and-thunder plays he was one of the headliners, his name familiar to theater goers all over the country. A few old-timers help him along.

Another bleary-eyed wretch staggers along forgotten by his former admirers, although one of his old songs is still occasionally heard. He was one of a famous variety team when Koster & Bial's place in 23rd Street was in its glory.

There is a saloon on the Bowery managed by an ex-actor where old-time thespians congregate.

Here may be found one who a few years ago was a clever blackface knockabout acrobat. A fur-lined overcoat, the last remnant of better times, hides his nakedness, for there is no coat or vest under it and he has but a fragment of a flannel shirt. Whisky gave him the nerve or courage to do his tricks, but it also brought on palsy. Now when he takes a drink he throws a towel around his neck, holds one end in the hand in which he holds the glass, and pulls the other end down with the disengaged hand. In this way the hand holding the glass is sufficiently steadied to be brought to his mouth. And as he formerly amused audiences, now he amuses his companions, who treat him for the peculiar pleasure they find in watching his contortions and antics as he takes his drink.

Another frequenter at this bar was a soloist in Thomas' orchestra, later an arranger of music. He sought the end of a rainbow. The rainbow was a beautiful singer who drank his wine, spent his money and sold the favors which he thought were reserved for him alone to others. When his money was gone the rainbow vanished and he became a misogynist. The deluded wretch found consolation in the stone fence, whisky and hard cider. From the Broadway cafés he went by rapid stages to the tough saloons of the Bowery, and is now a wreck making a bare living as "piano professor" in a dive.

Two other wrecks, once respected men, are often found in the same saloon. One was an inventor, who, though married, spent a fortune on other women. One of these introduced him to a more insidious enchanter—

absinthe. Under its influence he exchanged patent rights for women's smiles until he became penniless. Neglected by his family, forsaken by the women who robbed him, he also became a hater of women and is only faithful to the green demon when he can raise the price.

Another is a physician who is suffering from some painful affection for which he takes morphine. That is the reason he gives for taking the drug, but he did not come to Povertyville until his wife died, then he began to drink heavily, and when this did not suffice to drown his sorrow he took morphine. A friendly druggist supplies the drug and his relatives pay for his lodging and meals.

"Shadder," a sot known in every Park Row low saloon, died a few months ago. He had an unfailing daily income of half a dollar given him by a friend, which went over the bar. After his death it was found that he was a Yale graduate and the son of a millionaire. His companions and intimates were mostly college-bred men, but, like himself, sots.

There may be something fascinating in reading the lives of great criminals, but there is little of interest in the lives of the petty criminals of Povertyville. A few have, however, had curious careers.

One who began as a pickpocket on the Bowery became in time a notorious burglar and spent several terms in prison.

During his last term he suddenly announced that he would reform, and he has apparently carried out his intention. With the proceeds of his last burglary he bought a saloon on the Bowery and his place became the rendezvous of his former associates. After several arrests were made in his place he was accused of being a stool pigeon for the police, and his patronage decreased. The place was closed and the reformed burglar disappeared from the Bowery.

Some of the criminals are the black sheep of respectable families. One young man of this character is now working as a dishwasher in a Bowery restaurant. This fellow possesses an innate depravity which neither moral teachings, chastisement, a mother's pleading nor prison bars have been able to eradicate. From early youth he has sought the association of toughs and since his manhood he has made his home among the vicious and criminal classes of Povertyville. On rare occasions he visits members of his family, expresses deep contrition for his faults, and will then work for a few days or weeks. Suddenly he disappears and is next heard of in connection with some crime. A peculiarity in his case is that he always drinks heavily before committing a crime.

When in a contrite mood he works as a cook, waiter, piano player, or salesman. He is also a clever acrobat and actor when not under the influence of drink and as such he can earn far more than he has ever made as a criminal. He has the appearance of a criminal, and when drunk he is an ordinary sot. He has saved the reputation of his family, among whom are well-known professional men, by passing under an alias.

Another of these black sheep started near the top of the ladder and is now near the bottom. This fellow, a college graduate, had luxurious tastes and indulgent, wealthy parents. They overlooked his first offense, which was to forge his father's name to a check for a small amount with which he paid a bet. His next offense was in connection with another forgery, this time a check for a hundred dollars, which he gave to his mistress. She raised it to nine hundred dollars, and the parents could not prosecute her without involving the son. He was sent to Europe, where he was imprisoned for some offense committed there, then returned as a crooked gambler.

Here he became a drunkard, tried his hand again at forgery, and went to prison. Since then he has been a confidence man, a sneak thief and a pickpocket. Now he steals for his lodgings, meals and drinks. He prides himself upon the fact that he has never earned a dollar honestly.

There is a decrepit old fellow who picks up a scanty living as pool-room or gambling-house attendant and "tout" or professional tipster, who was for years a notorious dive keeper. He began as a barkeeper in a sporting saloon, took an interest in all forms of sport and later became a bookmaker. Then he opened a dive in the Tenderloin, but, the old fellow says, the protection money paid as the price of peace ate up the profits. When a high police official raised the price of peace, the dive keeper could not see the raise. This brought on a moral spasm in the official, who thereupon closed up the dive, leaving the keeper penniless. A few years later he was again at the old business, but his dive was now run so unobtrusively that only the initiated knew of its existence. Again the police drove him out and he disappeared until a few years ago, when he appeared as the manager of a Bowery dive.

This place was closed and the old dive keeper is now penniless and almost friendless.

Several former Bowery dive keepers have been equally unfortunate. One who had a dive in Chrystie Street and afterwards a concert hall on the Bowery paid all his profits to keep out of the clutches of the police. He was afterwards a manager for another dive, then a barker, and is now a tramp.

Especially hard has it gone with those who gave evidence against the police during the Lexow investigation which the State Legislature carried on in 1894.

One of these witnesses was afterwards hounded by the police of this and neighboring cities; place after place which he opened, or was supposed to have an interest in, was closed; even in a western city his application for a license was refused and he returned to New York without money or friends. He became a waiter at a seaside resort, finally drifting back to the old quarters near the Bowery. He is now a waiter or bartender in a Bowery saloon.

A similar fate overtook the keeper of a cider room and gambling house near the Bowery. This man was not a witness before the Lexow committee but was suspected of having given private information. As a result the cider room was closed, the gambling house overhead was raided, although running in the name of a club, and the man moved to Jersey City. A few summers ago he opened a small saloon at Coney Island, but closed it when he found the police determined to drive him out by compelling him to keep his place closed Sundays. His reputation as a "squealer" or informer had preceded him there as elsewhere, and he returned to New York, but could not obtain a license for a saloon nor did he dare to open a cider room. He became a waiter, working on roof gardens in summer and in dives in winter.

Truly, the way of the transgressor is hard, but not always.

One of the vilest of the Bowery dive keepers, the nephew of a prominent rabbi now deceased, hides his Jewish cognomen under an Irish alias. He has conducted vile resorts on and near the Bowery for twenty years, the police no sooner closing one than another was opened under the same management. This man has powerful political backing and a substantial bank account. He has never been arrested; indeed, it was said that when the police found it necessary to close his place as a sop to public opinion, they first notified him and gave him a chance to hire another store near his old place. His last place on the Bowery was closed by the police a few months ago, and he has now a place in the Tenderloin.

Occasionally there are sojourners in Povertyville— temporary wretches who go on periodical sprees, come to Povertyville where they are unknown, mingle with its wretches and plunge into its vices. During their stay they become vulgar, foul and besotten. They lead Dr. Jekyll and Mr. Hyde lives, their latter existence revolting to them in their sober periods, the former unknown to them in their periods of intoxication.

One of these shows up at regular intervals. He is not ordinarily a drinker, but he says he occasionally feels an uncontrollable desire to drink and after the first glass he continues to drink until insensible. Formerly when he felt the craving coming on he went to a hotel where he was known and, with a few bottles of whisky at his side, remained in his room for several days. The hotel physician then attended him until he became sober. Now, after he has started on a spree he goes to a Bowery lodging house, pays for a room for a week, leaves a few dollars with the keeper and starts out to drink heavily. He spends his waking hours in dives and morgues, associates with drunkards and vile women. If his money gives out before his craving is fully satisfied he will exchange his clothes for drink. During this time he is apparently ignorant of his normal self, calls himself by a fictitious name, and recalls incidents of former visits but nothing of his normal periods. At the end of his spree he goes back to his lodging house and then falls into a heavy sleep which lasts for a day or more. He leaves the house before he is fully sensible of his surroundings, generally at night, and returns home. The period of intoxication lasts from seven to ten days, his sober periods about six months. He says he has no recollection of himself after he has taken the first drink.

When he recovers, his experience appears to him like a jumbled dream.

(Such cases are not rare. Some years ago the writer saw a New York physician partly intoxicated in the negro quarter of a southern city. The physician denied his identity and said he was never in New York, and the writer supposed he had been mistaken. He afterwards visited the physician in New York and learned that the latter had left some friends with whom he had been drinking, to return to his home a few blocks away, but did not reach his home until two weeks later. He had no recollection of his actions during that time, and no clue to his whereabouts except his hat, which bore the name of a dealer in the city in which the writer had seen him.)

Among the female characters of Povertyville there are some who are not vulgar, a few who are not lewd.

The women are more sensitive than the men, drink little and lie outrageously. They are cynics, despising the men who buy their favors, yet willing to make a confidant of any liberal patron. They will tell him the pitiful story of their lives, every word of which is a falsehood, and will in return expect the confidence of the patron, to be afterwards used to blackmail him.

A serious obstacle in retracing the careers of the women is their many aliases and the many women who use the same name.

Those who come from higher circles adopt a new name in each stopping place, and some women may be known by several names at the same time. Under such circumstances it is almost impossible to gather anything of their history.

Among the exotics there are a few peculiar characters. In a Bowery dive there is a young woman whose face and form might serve as an artist's model, whose dress, deportment and speech show refinement, but whose vocation is little better than that of the women of the street. She gains a livelihood from commissions on drinks ordered by her admirers. Her own drink, sherry, costs 25 cents, half of which is her commission.

Although surrounded by depraved, vulgar wretches, her language is free from obscenity and vulgarity and she skillfully turns the conversation when proposals for her favors are made. When admirers become too ardent she puts them off with promises or turns them over to other women in the place. She is an adept at inventing pitiful tales about the women, and by arousing the sympathy and curiosity of the listener she induces him to select such other woman instead of herself. It is known that she has refused large sums of money for her favors.

Some say that she is a stool pigeon, others think she is the wife of the proprietor or of an employe. She says little about herself and every habitué will tell a different tale about her.

Most of the chaste women found in the disreputable resorts are the wives of waiters. They sit there under the watchful eye of their husbands, drinking with strangers for commissions.

Occasionally one of the exotics is recognized by one of a slumming party, but the woman is discreet and the man, who may have enjoyed her favors under more congenial surroundings, says nothing. On rare occasions one is recognized by a father, a brother, or a deceived husband. Then Povertyville has a sensation.

One woman, whose history can be traced back, began her career in Povertyville, rose to a high position in fast life, and is now back in her old haunts again.

About twenty years ago she was in a police court charged with assault upon her stepmother, and was sent to a reformatory, where she was thrown in contact with depraved women and learned their ways.

After her release she went to a Bowery dive, then to a concert hall, and later she was a member of a burlesque company. About 1890 she was in the chorus of a Broadway theater and soon afterwards she became the mistress of a government official. For a few years she was a familiar figure in Saratoga and Long Branch, and had at her command all the luxuries money could procure.

A few years ago she was well known in the Tenderloin district, and now she is back on the Bowery. Dissipation has made her repulsive, but she still has admirers, attracted, without doubt, by her brilliant conversation.

Two cases were reported in the press a short time ago of women who once moved in good circles and descended into the whirlpool of Povertyville.

One of these closed her career in the slums within five years after leaving her home. The daughter of a military officer, well reared, with a good voice, pretty face and fine figure, she sought fame before the footlights. Three years ago she was one of the prettiest girls in the chorus of a Broadway theater, with scores of admirers. One of these induced her to give up her position and live with him. In a year she became a drunkard and an opium fiend, her lover discarded her and she began her downward career. In less than two years she had run the gamut from the most luxurious house of ill fame in the Tenderloin to the Bowery dive and a miserably furnished room in Povertyville. There is another wretch of whom interesting scraps of history are known. She was the wife of a musician in a theater orchestra. She learned that he visited a dive near the theater after his work was done, and found him there one night. Without creating a scene she attracted his attention and the couple left together. A few days later she found him there again with a female companion, but this time she took a seat at his table and ordered drinks. He created a scene and was ordered out by the bouncer, while she remained, drank with strangers and accompanied one of them to a furnished room house. This was her introduction to a life of vice. At one time she was arrested for soliciting and sent for her husband, who secured her release. She was not heard of for a few years, then turned up in a Tenderloin dance hall with the son of a well-to-do merchant, a fellow hardly out of his teens. During the World's Fair in Chicago she had a "ladies' boarding house" there and her cards were found in every gambling house and in many hotels in that city. Later she appeared as co-respondent in a divorce suit in Chicago, then again in the Tenderloin, where she was frequently arrested for robbing patrons. Now, old, haggard, a drunken sot, she is either on the Bowery or in prison. There is one old wretch, though still young looking under the gas light, who has the scar of a gash across her cheek, which a thick coating of chalk and rouge cannot hide. When under the influence of drink she becomes loquacious and speaks of a wedding trip around the world in 1873 and 1874. She will describe the Vienna exposition of 1873, her escape from Madrid in the fall of that year when the Virginius affair made life disagreeable for Americans in Spain, her trip through Egypt, India, China and Hawaii. She knows every part of this country, but will not speak of California, from which state she probably came. Even in her most loquacious mood she avoids every reference to her family and it is impossible to draw her out in conversation.

One vile wretch who came from Hamburg in charge of a procuress about ten years ago, can blaspheme in several languages, always introducing foulness and obscenity.

She speaks fluently German, French, Russian and Hungarian, plays the piano and is well educated. She has no conception of natural modesty, but speaks of it as an artificial sentiment which involves personal restrictions. She is attractive in appearance, honest and kind, but the total lack of that womanly modesty and her persistently foul language make her repellant.

One, a newcomer, although past middle age, is probably driven to her calling through want. She is evidently a cultured woman, neat, far more cleanly than most of the wretches of the street, speaks German and French fluently and without vulgarity.

She is shy, as though not accustomed to the life she is leading, drinks little and has no lover. Those who have been with her say that she wears a cross suspended from her neck, and prays before retiring. She is extremely reticent, has no friends, and no one knows her history.

There is little romance in the lives of the women of Povertyville who live by crime rather than by vice. Almost all are mistresses of petty thieves, adding to the common fund by shoplifting. The careers of most of these women are alike. They are indigenous wretches who frequented tough balls and there met their first lovers. After consorting with them they took up furnished rooms and became acquainted with professional criminals. In this way they learned the "art" of stealing, especially shoplifting. When they make a big haul they move out of Povertyville and then look for bigger game. If shoplifting has not been profitable the woman will look for patrons in dives. Only one is known to have a curious criminal history. She was the friend or mistress of a western sport whom she robbed, and came to New York. Here she became the companion of a criminal, her special business being blackmail.

Through equivocally worded newspaper personals she obtained a number of compromising letters and lived in luxury on the weakness of her victims. One of the latter informed a friendly police official and this woman was arrested and after passing through what she called "the third degree" she gave up all the incriminating letters and was discharged. She and her partner next tried the badger game, but he was soon arrested for an old

THE WRETCHES

offense and she took up shoplifting and robbing patrons who sought her favors. One of these had her arrested and she was sent to prison. Upon her release she continued upon her criminal career, first in the Tenderloin, gradually coming down until she reached the Bowery, where drink and disease are carrying her off. She has been in prison several times, always on one of two charges—shoplifting or larceny. Some say she is a minister's daughter.

Before closing this chapter we will follow the career of one wretch whom the writer knew for several years. This man studied for the ministry, then he took up the study of medicine, and after he graduated he married and settled down in his native town in New Hampshire. On a visit to New York he formed the acquaintance of a young woman who gave him an opportunity to do her some trifling service. She told him a pitiful tale of desertion and of a cousin, a stock broker, who supported her, aroused the doctor's sympathy and he aided her and promised to visit her again. A few weeks later he came to New York again, saw the woman, and this time they become more intimate. He soon found an excuse for coming to New York once or twice a week, and finally, telling his wife he was going to Europe, he made his home with the woman. She had induced him to invest money in stocks, her cousin acting as broker, but when his money was gone he found that the stock was worthless and he could not raise a dollar on what he had paid thousands. To cap his discomfiture the woman told him the stock broker was her husband. The doctor threatened to kill him, and when the stock broker entered the room the doctor drew a pistol, fired a shot at the man, and escaped without waiting to see that the shot was wasted. Six months later his wife received a letter from the Brazilian government informing her that her husband, a surgeon in the Brazilian army, was wounded and lay in the hospital at Rio Janeiro. He had been awarded a medal for bravery in an action with rebels, but had received several wounds from which it was thought he would die. She went to Rio Janeiro, was by his side until he recovered, then she sickened and died. He had in the meantime begun to take morphine and after his wife's death he became a drug fiend. A year later he had charge of a drug store on the east side in this city, and there he married again. Through a remarkable freak of fate his old flame came again in his way. He had never before gone out of his store without his morphine, but this day he was on the west side and finding that he had forgotten his drug, went into a drug store to get some. As he went out his former sweetheart entered, there was a mutual recognition and his infatuation for her returned. She had never been in that drug store before, and it seems peculiar that both should be drawn at the same time to this store, miles away from their homes. Such is fate.

The broker had discarded her and the doctor resumed his former relations, now leading a double life—a life of poverty and misery with his wife, a life of luxury and pleasure with this woman. But neither the income from his store nor from an illegal medical practice sufficed to supply two households and his craving for morphine. He lost his position, was fined for illegal practice, his wife secured a divorce and when he had no more money the other woman had no further use for him. He became a homeless outcast, gave bestial exhibitions to obtain money for liquor and morphine and did not hesitate to steal. One day the woman who was responsible for all his misfortunes met him on the Bowery. She, too, had reached the lowest level. She gave him a dollar she had just earned—all she had—and he bought enough morphine to end his life.

Readers may remember the account of a suicide in a lodging house, who left a note containing a parody on the lines, "Goodbye, Proud World, I Am Going Home," and some cynical reflections upon the uselessness of living when life's pleasures cease. Such was the end of this wretch.

CHAPTER V

SLAVES OF THE PIPE.

OF ALL the wretches of Povertyville none reach that height of bliss, nor descend to that depth of misery, that falls to the lot of the opium smoker. None are less to be envied in their happiness, less to be pitied in their wretchedness.

We must pity the unfortunate who has received an opiate in some medicine and finds that he cannot obtain relief from physical suffering without it. He may be taking the drug for years unconscious of the fact that he is the victim of the drug habit.

For the slave of the pipe there are no extenuating circumstances. He knows its dangers when he takes the first whiff, he becomes conscious of its seductive properties when he feels like trying it again, and every step from the time he smokes his first pill until he has become a confirmed fiend carries with it a warning. When he has reached that stage where the drug becomes a necessity he is oblivious to warnings, indifferent to its effects, unwilling to forego its pleasures, unable to withstand its cravings. Under its effects he is in elysium; without it, the torments of hell could not surpass his sufferings.

A PELL STREET OPIUM JOINT.

Read "De Quincey's Confessions of an Opium Eater" if you would know the abject misery of the wretch to whom the drug is like the air of life when he is without it.

But De Quincey never knew the blissful contentment which follows a few whiffs from the pipe.

The frightful craving for "hop," as they call the prepared paste of opium used by smokers, is like the gasping for air of the poor devil strangling on the gallows. The sudden transition to happiness when the fiend has had a few whiffs from the pipe, not even the happiness of Maxmilian Morell, when he met his Valentine in Monte Cristo's cave, can compare with it.

Hop smoking is an expensive vice. It drains the pocket and it drains the mental, moral and physical powers. It drives away care and those human instincts which create care. When he needs the drug he must get it. He is no longer restrained by the still, soft voice within, not even by that instinct which compelled old Adam to make breeches out of fig leaves, as the Breeches Bible tells us.

Body and soul for a thimbleful of hop; with it he leaves the world to you; he has heaven.

Opium dulls the physical and mental sensibilities, and the fiend apparently becomes inured to hardship, to hunger, cold, exposure and privation. The system, however, becomes more readily affected by disease, while his dulled sensibilities and weakened brain do not arouse in him a realization of his condition. He may be starving, yet have no desire for food; he may be in the last stage of consumption, yet he will disregard the most urgent symptoms as though unconscious of them.

His life is a dream, a horrible nightmare when without his hop, a dream of bliss when drawing on the pipe.

It is not, however, except in the novice, a dream of air castles. It is a Nirvana-like repose, in which there is no consciousness of self or surroundings.

The confirmed fiend lies on his cot "cooking" or preparing the pellets of hop mechanically, conscious of the hop jar, lamp, and hook next to him, but otherwise oblivious to surroundings, to the flight of time, to the demands of nature. It is a mistaken idea that opium smoking produces lascivious dreams. When one tries it for the first time the mind is occupied with observations upon the impressions produced.

The mind is more active and alert than usual and concentrated upon expected effects; the mental impressions are, however, invariably agreeable. There is a feeling of physical ease such as one experiences when smoking a good cigar after a hearty dinner.

After smoking a few pills the novice becomes drowsy, falls into a dreamless sleep and awakes with a dull headache.

The novice is tempted to try it again, not because there is any desire for the drug, but because he wishes to repeat the pleasant experience just before falling asleep. After the novelty has worn off and before he has become a habitual smoker he may build air castles while smoking, but in whatever direction the mind wanders the pictures are pleasant, and though exaggerated and elaborated to please the fancy, they present themselves with the vividness of actualities.

The actor will dream of success on the stage, extended until he sees himself the center of the scene, the only actor on the stage, with the applause of thousands ringing in his ears.

The gambler will dream of a game in which he holds the winning hand, the strongest hand possible, his opponents chipping in until the stakes reach the ceiling. So, too, the mechanic dreams of wonderful inventions, the merchant of extraordinary sales, the artist of grand conceptions. Only the roué whose waking thoughts are of women will dream of them when under the influence of opium. The dream lasts until the smoker falls asleep. It is not a true dream but a mental aberration, during which the victim is indifferent to what is going on around him, even threatened danger failing to arouse him after he has smoked a few pills.

At a later stage the victim notes a desire to smoke and a feeling of malaise when the desire is unsatisfied.

The pipe dreams become less vivid and more complicated and after a time they must be conjured up, the victim making an effort to concentrate his mind upon the subject. As the smoker becomes a "fiend," as the person afflicted with the drug habit is called, the power to think while smoking is lost. He gradually increases the number of pills, smoking thirty or more at a sitting, the interval between the sittings decreasing until only a few hours may elapse between them. In these intervals he sleeps or attends to business, but as his mental and physical powers wane he becomes a complete wreck. After a few hours from the last smoke the craving begins again. The mind is centered upon his want, an indescribably intense desire which nothing but the drug or death can appease.

He will beg, steal, do anything to obtain hop; if he cannot obtain it the frightful craving increases, and a series of pathological symptoms begins. He yawns and sneezes. Pains in every bone, joint and muscle set in and an agonizing pain is felt in the spinal cord. This pain is likened to the suffering from an exposed nerve of a decayed tooth, a thousandfold intensified. The whole cord feels as if it were exposed and molten lead poured upon it. At the same time he suffers from prostration and restlessness, constantly moving about in search of ease. In this condition he will not hesitate to commit murder or suicide to obtain relief, but he is too weak to overcome a child. His throat burns and a gnawing pain at the stomach sets in, followed by retching and vomiting. The frightful agony produced by this combination of symptoms reaches its height on the second or third day after deprivation. Suddenly his mind gives way or he falls in a state of collapse in which he dies.

Such is the end of the confirmed habitué when his funds are exhausted. Most die, however, of consumption, the usual complication following the prolonged use of the drug.

When one has taken the drug but a short time and is suddenly deprived of it, the painful symptoms are less severe, but the sickening retching and vomiting are more persistent. The constitution has, however, not been so seriously undermined and there is less danger of collapse. The mind sometimes gives way; usually, however, after the combination of symptoms have continued for two or three days they gradually subside and in a few days more they disappear. There is no further desire for the drug.

Whether the drug be taken in the form of opium or morphine, whether taken internally, hypodermically or by inhalation through the pipe, the agony produced by its deprivation is the same, but the most pleasurable effects are produced by smoking. This is the only form in which more is used than is necessary to satisfy the craving; it is the most alluring, the most expensive form and the form in which the mental and physical powers are most quickly weakened, but the smoker never dies from an overdose of the drug, as sometimes happens when it is used in other ways.

The smoker, when he has the means, will fit up a small den in his home, where he can gratify his passion in secret or in company with a few congenial companions.

For a time he can continue the vice without betraying himself except to other smokers. Burning hop gives off a heavy, penetrating and persistent odor which is instantly recognized by one accustomed to it, and the smoker has the odor about him for hours after a sitting. After he has become a confirmed fiend his appearance betrays him. The ashy complexion, tensely drawn skin over the forehead and the infallible sign—extremely small "pin-hole" pupils, making the colored iris more prominent, with glassy whites tinged often with yellow—cannot be concealed. One of the finger tips of the left hand is colored a deep brown, produced by frequently touching the pill while "cooking" to see if it is of the proper consistency. In manner the fiend is listless, becoming restless when the craving comes on.

The recent novitiate into this vice is mentally brighter and more alert than formerly, but as the habit grows his mind becomes weakened and this is usually the first change noticed by his friends.

Chinatown seems to possess a fascination for opium smokers. They will visit it at night, feast in its restaurants and fill up their dens with Chinese ornaments. Some fit up dens in Chinatown—furnish them with a medley of Chinese and American furniture, a couch replacing the bed, a Chinese lantern instead of a lamp, and Chinese ornaments strewn about and dangling from the ceiling.

When the smoker is near the end of his resources he will hire a small room, perhaps a corner of a Chinaman's

OPIUM JOINT KEEPER.

room, and make a bunk out of a table or some boards placed upon barrels. Some old clothes, rags or a bundle of straw forms the head rest. This is then his bed, table, chair and all the furniture he has any use for. At first he will have a curtain around his bunk to shield him from inquisitive eyes; later he is indifferent. When hard pressed for money he will rent out the space over his head for another bunk and may even rent part of his own bunk, making his living room but little larger than the coffin he will soon occupy.

There are many women in Povertyville addicted to the pipe. They are almost without exception lewd women, either connected with the stage or with brothels, or else they are the consorts of criminals. The constant use of the drug destroys in them the moral sense and the sexual appetite.

During the early period of their slavery to the drug they will fit up dens in their homes or in Chinatown. Later on when they have no means to obtain hop and their companions will not supply them they will consort with Chinamen, living with them as their wives. There are many such white wives of Chinamen in Pell, Mott and Doyer streets, the heart of Chinatown. Their rooms are scrupulously clean, cleanliness being, perhaps, the only virtue the Chinaman insists upon in his wife. Otherwise the rooms are poorly furnished, bunks or long tables being the most notable furniture. Occasionally there is a kitchen table, a chair and a stove. Meals are usually taken at one of the restaurants in the neighborhood, not one of the elaborate show places which slumming parties visit, but a place patronized mainly by Chinamen.

So these wretched creatures live, two or three with their yellow-skinned husbands occupying one room, leading an indolent existence, dozing, dreaming, unconcerned about their fast-ebbing lives.

The smoking outfit consists of the pipe, lamp, needle, pipe bowl cleaner, sponge, a small bowl to hold water, hop jar, and ash receiver. The hop is the extract of opium prepared for smoking by a secret process which the whites have not fully mastered. A few druggists have succeeded in making an imitation which will deceive white smokers but not Chinamen. It looks like a thick, black, pasty salve. The best quality, number one, is made from opium. Number two is number one mixed with opium ash.

The pipe or Heen cheung is a heavy bamboo stem about two feet long and an inch in diameter without mouthpiece, except an ivory tip, and a clay bowl inserted near one end of the stem. The bowl is closed at the top, having only a pin hole opening in the center of the top, upon which the pill is placed while smoking. The lamp is somewhat like an alcohol lamp, burning peanut oil. The needle or yen hok is merely a short knitting needle, sometimes with a handle. The jar or hop toy is a little china or horn box about two inches high, the shape of a salve box or thimble, in which the hop is kept. The ash

THE WRETCHES

receiver is an ordinary shallow dish, sometimes a clam shell, on which the ashes are collected. The ashes are sold, being used to make a poorer quality of hop.

When a smoker gets a "yin" or craving he lies down on his couch with the little lamp burning by his side. With the yen hok he draws out from the jar a quantity of the paste about the size of a pea. Then he "cooks" the hop by twirling it on the end of the needle over the flame of the lamp. It sputters and boils like boiling tar or sealing wax, but it does not catch fire and its color changes from black to dark orange. It gradually acquires a more solid consistency, losing its stickiness, and this is frequently tested on the tip of the finger. The mass is then "chyed" or drawn into strings by being placed upon the bowl, then drawn out by the needle, twirled around the needle and again cooked. In this way the whole mass is subjected to the heat. When it is about as dense as glazier's putty and does not stick, the pill is considered cooked. It is then rolled into a pill, placed over the hole in the bowl, lighted in the flame of the lamp while the smoker draws on the stem. He does not emit the smoke as he would when smoking tobacco, but he inhales the fumes from the smouldering pill until it is entirely consumed. The habitué may consume a pill in one draw; the novice stops after each whiff. The pill at once ceases to burn and in relighting it the flavor is destroyed, as it is mixed with the flavor of the peanut oil. The expert takes long whiffs with slight intervals, consuming a pill in two or three minutes. He will smoke ten to fifteen pills an hour.

The odor of burning hop is heavy, oppressive, and in a close room nauseating. In the open air it is not unpleasant. Judging from the statements of druggists the number of drug habitués is enormous, many taking opium or one of its preparations or derivatives in the form of medicine for years. Those who use the drug knowingly take it in its pure state either as opium pill or powder, or as laudanum, or take morphine in pill or powder or through the hypodermic syringe. It is a strange fact that most of this class of habitués are physicians, druggists and hospital attendants, men who know the disastrous effects of the drug.

Most of the smokers are men with much leisure time —actors, sports, panders and criminals.

In a narrow street leading to the Bowery there are a number of dens or "joints" fitted up for smokers, where they can "hit the pipe," as they call opium smoking, without interference.

In one house, the exterior of which is like a poor, dirty tenement, there are scores of such dens, most of them kept by Chinamen, some by negroes, a few by whites. Some large rooms hold from four to eight bunks. Some rooms, or rather closets, have one bunk filling the room.

They say that one of these small rooms is rented to a popular actor who spends his Sundays and holidays

COCAINE AND OPIUM DEALER AND FIEND.

here, bringing his layout in a satchel in the early morning hours and departing in the carriage that brought him the following morning. He does not mingle with the "regulars," does not patronize the Chinese restaurants, and when entering and departing from the house will not acknowledge a greeting, although there seems to be no question concerning his identity.

It is not unusual to see carriages stop at night before this and other houses in the neighborhood, deposit their white occupants, who hurry into the building, and return for them in a few hours or the next evening. Those who still possess a sense of shame come in a hired cab and carry their layout in a satchel. These have private rooms or dens. Later on, when they cannot hide their vice from other smokers, they will find companions with whom they have a room in company, or will go together to a Chinaman's apartment. Women generally come in pairs in hired cabs and go to Chinamen's rooms.

In a tenement reeking with filth and vice, crowded with Chinamen with a sprinkling of blacks and whites, there lives a woman who has fitted up a fairy palace in a human cesspool. Carpeted floor, lace curtains over windows the shutters of which are rarely opened, Chinese ornaments hanging from the ceiling, oriental bric-a-brac, and an ornamental Chinese lantern with a colored shade throwing a pink tinge over all—such are the furnishings of this room. On a couch in a cozy corner, shut in by China silk screens, this woman lies dozing, perhaps dreaming, inhaling the fumes of hop.

She is about thirty years old, has beautiful features, is tall and well built. She is an adept in the use of cosmetics and unguents, for under their use there is no indication of sallowness of the cheeks, her eyes are brilliant, the pupils being artificially dilated with belladonna. She is refined and well educated, and evidently accustomed to cultured, perhaps fashionable, society. They say she rarely goes out by day, but occasionally goes away in a carriage at night, taking her layout with her. Her meals are brought in from a Chinese restaurant.

Some who think they know say she was an actress before she became a fiend, while others who think they know say she is the divorced wife of a San Francisco merchant. She takes far better care of herself than most female fiends.

Nearby is another den, not so elaborately fitted up, the inmate of which is more interesting than the other. This is a young woman, probably a southerner, who makes a good living by showing visitors how to "hit the pipe."

Either she has not reached that stage where sallowness, emaciation and pine-hole pupils become marked, or else she is able to hide these unmistakable signs of the vice, for she is plump, there is a ruddy glow on her dark skin not due to the red lantern shade, and her pupils are

COCAINE FIEND.

but slightly contracted. She is jolly, a rare trait in the confirmed smoker. She is refined in manner and speech, prefers to speak French and does not fear recognition. She explains every detail of the process, cooks a pill, smokes it, and offers the pipe to visitors.

She adds the statement made and probably believed by every smoker that the habit can be given up at any time. None have the will power to do so when it has once become a habit.

Visitors pay whatever they wish for the exhibition, placing the money on the mantle.

The only redeeming feature in the career of the pipe fiends, though an uncharitable view it be, is the shortness of their useless lives. Consumption generally sets in and carries them off.

Many of the opium fiends are also "coke" fiends or cocaine habitués. This drug is snuffed up the nose and produces a mild stimulation, followed by intense depression. Scores of such "coke" fiends live in the poor lodging houses near Chinatown. A basement pool room near Chatham Square is the hang-out for these wretches.

A word might here be said about Chinese restaurants. These have increased to a remarkable extent and are now found in all parts of the city. Most of these outside of Chinatown are patronized by whites and negroes.

These are poor imitations of real Chinese restaurants, most are conducted by whites and have white cooks but have Chinese waiters. The dishes are intended to suit.

the taste of the whites, only two, yakomen and chop suey, being prepared according to Chinese methods. The former is a noodle soup containing bits of chicken, pork and eggs. The latter is a porridge of beans, onions, mushrooms, sprouts, pork and chicken, highly seasoned.

The pretentious restaurants of Chinatown, those shown to slumming parties, are elaborately fitted up. One has tables and chairs of ebony, inlaid with mother of pearl, silverware, fine chinaware, and for white visitors knives, forks and spoons and a bill of fare printed in Chinese and English. Cleanliness, neatness and decorum are not surpassed in the fashionable restaurants of Fifth Avenue.

The rank and file of Chinamen, however, go to small restaurants which are rarely visited by whites, except fiends who live in the neighborhood. High stools are used instead of chairs and the tables are a little higher and but little larger than the stools.

There are no ornaments, no silverware, there is heavy crockery, and everybody handles the quitsees or chop sticks. A plate of chop suey or yakomen costs here ten cents and is sufficient for a meal. Tea is served instead of water in all Chinese restaurants. Though irrelevant to the subject of this chapter, we will mention here the special features of Chinatown. These are the theater, restaurants, Joss House or Temple, the opium joints, gambling houses and business houses. All slumming parties visit the theater, which has been described.

Guides take visitors to a Chinese restaurant, either the one at the corner of Pell Street and the Bowery, on Pell Street opposite Doyer Street, corner Doyer Street and the Bowery, or on Mott Street in the Joss House. These differ as much from the ordinary Chinese retaurants as a Fifth Avenue restaurant differs from a Bowery "hash house." There is little difference in the Chinese opium joints, and when whites open joints they imitate the Chinamen and add a lot of Chinese ornaments, which they scatter about the room. The Joss House in Mott Street near Chatham Square is as interesting as any other feature in Chinatown and is shown to visitors. It has been so often described, pictured and visited that it ought to be familiar to all readers. The gambling houses are run openly but are rarely visited by whites, and sightseers are not welocme. The game stops as soon as a party of whites enter and the visitors see only a few round tables, high stools and a number of chattering Chinamen.

Opposite the theater is the notorious Chatham Club. Near the Joss House is a notorious dive which has been frequently raided. Its back room is patronized mainly by lewd women who have contracted the opium habit and their lovers.

Near the theater is the Rescue Mission, which is crowded nightly by the wretches of Povertyville and is one of the sights of Chinatown.

CHAPTER VI

THE LIVES OF THE WRETCHES.

THE wretches of Povertyville keep no diary, for to them yesterday is but a bitter memory, and could they command forgetfulness the moment past would be as veiled to them as the ages to come. To know how they live we must follow their footsteps.

There is the poor devil who came to this city in search of work. Without a trade except perhaps farming, unaccustomed to indoor labor, with limited education, he has been unable to secure steady employment. Now, without money or friends, clothes shabby, ambition almost extinguished, we find him in a cheap lodging house.

He has learned to beg but he has still some manhood left and would rather work.

He is awakened at six o'clock, the attendant rapping at the door of his seven-by-five closet, or shaking him as he lies on his cot in the dormitory.

He throws off the horse blanket with which he is covered, dresses, washes at the common lavatory, uses the comb and brush chained to the faucet, brushes his clothes with a whisk broom and his shoes with his coat sleeve, then goes off in search of work. After scanning the "help wanted" list clipped from the daily papers and posted before the Y. M. C. A. Building on the Bowery and several other places nearby, he begins the heart-breaking chase from place to place where help is wanted.

"Where did you work last?" "On a farm."
"References?" "Have none."
"Where do you live?" "In a Bowery lodging house."

No experience, no references, no home; three unsurmountable obstacles. Scores of times he has been told they would let him know and he has learned that this is a virtual rejection. Wherever he applies an hour later he is told "just too late." He has now another wasted day before him and another dreary wait for the morrow.

Our poor wretch has become accustomed to get along without breakfast and he spends the morning hours in the reading room of the Cooper Union or some other reading room in the neighborhood. At noon he makes his way to one of the many saloons on the Bowery and during the busy hour when the bar and free lunch counter are crowded he mingles with the crowd and gets a free meal, breakfast and dinner combined.

Then comes the task of the day to secure his "hote" money for his night's lodging. This means a begging or borrowing expedition. Men of this class who have no assured means of repaying loans do not obtain them readily and unless there is a newcomer at his lodging house he will be obliged to depend upon the generosity of sympathetic strangers. If he is an adept at reading faces and knows the tricks of the pan-handlers he will obtain enough to tide him over a few days. In the evening he will go to a mission where food is furnished after the services, join in the singing, and after receiving a cup of coffee and some bread he returns to his lodging house.

The next day there may be a variation in the routine. After the usual morning hunt for work if he has a few cents to spare he will play cards in his lodging house until noon hour is past. He will then go to the same saloon he visited the day before, buy a glass of beer and carry it to the free lunch counter. This is done to show the lunch man that he is a regular patron of the place, and he can pursue the course of the previous day for several days thereafter.

The afternoon is spent in a reading room or at the lodging house unless his funds are exhausted. Then he must go on another begging expedition.

These two days comprise the routine of life at an early stage of the wretch.

Let us now follow the wretch in his last stage.

The public comfort house in Mulberry Bend Park is one of the places where he spends his nights. In summer a park bench is his bed, but during the cold winter months a tender-hearted keeper will permit him to remain in this warm room, where he sleeps standing or leaning against his neighbor.

THE WRETCHES

Perhaps for days he has not removed his ragged coat or old shoes. Water is an abomination to him. Gladly would he request the judge to commit him to prison for ten days beginning two days before Christmas, but the dreadful ordeal of an enforced bath deters him. The ten days include a Christmas dinner, a New Year's dinner and one or two Sundays of idleness, but it also includes a wash.

If hydrophobia were merely a dread of water this wretch would have it in its most pronounced form.

At daybreak the keeper of the comfort house turns the wretch out. No time is lost in dressing, washing, or prayers, but off he goes to the Bowery for his breakfast. He may have secured a loaf of bread in the bread line the night before, or he may depend upon a free lunch counter in return for sweeping out the saloon.

Next comes the serious work of the day—to find some luckless individual who, after a night's carousal, has fallen asleep in a hallway or alleyway. If he finds one whose pockets are turned inside out he knows that a waiter has forestalled him. In that case the victim has probably been drugged and it is safe to remove his coat and shoes without awakening him. If the victim has not yet been "touched" or robbed the wretch makes a haul. He disposes of the proceeds to a bartender, investing the cash for beer, never for clothing. He drinks so much that he is overcome, is cleaned out and thrown out, and is next carried to the police station. If he has not made a haul he knows several tricks by which he can arouse sympathy and gain a few nickels and dimes. All go for beer. When he can gain nothing by trickery he will walk the streets till midnight, then go to the Bowery Mission, where coffee and bread are distributed, and later to Fleischman's corner, where he gets a loaf of bread. The day is spent in a "tub" house or walking the streets.

Occasionally he will go to a mission house, announce his willingness to reform, give his testimony, pose as the horrible example, be prayed over, cried over by tender-hearted and tender-minded evangelists, receive useless religious advice, some food and perhaps a ticket for a night's lodging. This he sells for the price of a glass of beer, and when that is consumed he returns to his sleeping place in the park. In warm weather he will "carry the banner," i. e., walk the streets all night.

Let us next follow an unfortunate fellow who retains his self-respect, who will not beg, borrow or steal, who is not suffering from hydrophobia, kleptomania, or any other of these moral perversions which are vices in Povertyville but diseases in Uppertendom.

This fellow wants work and will do any honest work, however menial, to keep him from starving. When he has the price he stops at the Mills Hotel, paying 20 cents for his room and 35 cents a day for his meals. If he has no money and no work he applies at the Bowery branch of the Y. M. C. A. Here, if he has references,

THE WRETCHES

he will receive bed and food for a few days while the superintendent aids him to procure work.

Or he will go to the Charity Organization Society on 22nd Street and he will be sent to the Wayfarers' Lodge on West 28th Street. He will there saw wood for three or four hours and he will receive therefor bed, bath and meals.

The society will also aid him to secure work. He might go to the Industrial Christian Alliance in Bleecker Street, where he can obtain temporary lodging and meals, doing work therefor, but that institution is rather a reformatory, most of its inmates being fallen men. Our case will find this place uncongenial and he will probably not remain more than a day.

As a last resort he will go to the Municipal lodging house.

He has one alternative—to walk the streets all night, stopping at the Bowery Mission at midnight for supper and at Fleischman's for the dole of bread which will serve him for next morning's breakfast. Our wretch does his own mending and his own laundry work. Instead of a white shirt he may wear a celluloid shirt front and none can tell the difference. Rubber collars and cuffs last for months and require no washing. At a barber school he obtains a free shave and haircut, the pupils using such material to practice upon. When not at work he goes to a reading room, the rendezvous of the homeless and unemployed.

When out of work for a lengthy period, when driven to the verge of despair, and beggary or theft seem to be the only resources left, this wretch goes to the police court and asks to be committed to the workhouse as a vagrant. Such cases are not rare.

The vicious and criminal classes live far different lives from the foregoing.

The fellow inbred in vice has no idea of virtue. The world owes him a living and he will collect the debt, appealingly or forcibly, but he will not work for it.

In many cases a female wretch supplies him with funds and he in return protects her. She has a furnished room which is his home. He appears on the street in the afternoon, goes to a show, a sporting resort or a club where others of his class congregate. There they gamble, but they play honestly, for each one suspects the others and all know the usual tricks. When the lamps are lit in the evening his work begins. His female companion appears on the street, and he follows her into the dive, where he sits behind her ready to receive anything she can steal from an unsuspecting victim. If the latter finds that he has been robbed nothing can be found on the woman.

If she takes a victim to her room he is there before they arrive, secretes himself in a closet or under the bed and waits for an opportunity to search the victim's clothes. If he makes a haul the woman is apprised of the fact and she dresses quickly and hurries away. When the victim finds that he has been robbed he hurries after her and she may be arrested, but nothing is found upon her, and the victim will rather stand the loss than the notoriety attached to publicity.

If the wretch has had no opportunity to rob the victim he waits until the latter leaves, then takes the money the woman has just earned, and the two get dinner, after which they go out for new victims. This is the routine of the pander. Sooner or later he goes to jail and after his release he becomes a full-fledged criminal.

The life of the criminal is much like the life of the pander. Nearly every one of the professional criminals has his "Moll" or female companion with whom he has a furnished room or flat. There is a social status among the criminals as strictly drawn as in higher life. Sooner would a portrait painter admit the sign dauber to his class or the society woman admit her cook to her four o'clock tea, than would the burglar or forger associate with the pickpocket or sneak thief.

This condition prevails even among the small fry of Povertyville. The pickpocket and the fellow whose game is hallway and gutter drunks hang about dives and low saloons while their "Molls" ply their trade on the street or do a little shoplifting.

When not engaged in criminal pursuits this class spends it days at the bar of a saloon or in gambling.

The criminal who looks for bigger game than door mats, handkerchiefs, children and gutter drunks, does not frequent dives and low saloons. His "Moll" is a professional shoplifter, and need not walk the streets or hang about for victims. The couple lead apparently respectable lives in a flat or furnished room, unsuspected until one of them is caught by the police. He spends his days in the more pretentious saloons, in the clubs, gambling houses or pool rooms, while she is working the department stores. He gives his occupation as "speculator," and this must satisfy inquisitive ones who want to know why he is out late at nights. Many of this class are opium fiends.

Of the female wretches of Povertyville the few virtuous unmarried ones who are not drug fiends find shelter in the woman's lodging houses or in furnished rooms. A score or more of philanthropic organizations look after the welfare of women if they are willing to work. When homeless and penniless they go to the Free Home for Girls in Mulberry Street, where there is no restriction to age, race, or nationality. The Charity Organization Society also provides for them temporarily if they are willing to work. As a last resort they go to the Salvation Army, or to the Municipal lodging house. Such women have little difficulty in obtaining work through one of the many employment bureaus in the city.

Most of the women who ply their trade on the street lead very regular lives. They, with their lovers or panders, live in furnished rooms in houses where no questions are asked. The woman rises in the afternoon, prepares breakfast in her room, then lounges about until evening. When darkness sets in she starts out in search of victims. Two women generally go together, with their lovers behind them. They go from dive to dive, sitting a few minutes in each, or saunter along the street, ever on the lookout to catch the eye of a possible patron. When one is caught and disposed of, the woman and her lover have dinner.

In the early morning hours, when the street and dives are deserted, they return to their rooms. This is the routine of their lives. Some lead apparently respectable lives, working as milliners or seamstresses by day. These have great difficulty in maintaining their double vocations and either break down from the strain or give up the day work altogether.

Those who have furnished rooms with respectable families claim to be waitresses or cashiers in all-night restaurants. These have no lovers. They do not bring their patrons to their homes but take them to a Raines Law hotel. Some live at these hotels, doing the chamber work in the morning, resting in the afternoon and walking the street at night.

Those in the "Ladies' Boarding Houses" lead dull, regular lives. Arising at noon, they have breakfast, fix up their rooms, read or sew till seven o'clock, then comes dinner. After that they are ready for visitors. They sit in the parlor awaiting admirers until the early morning hour, when they retire. They rarely leave the house unless hired for a night.

When the wretch has reached that stage where no artifice will enable her to secure patronage she joins the "Bazimer" colony or "fire lighters." These are old women who congregate at certain corners east of the Bowery waiting to be engaged to do a day's washing or scrubbing, and to light lamps and start fires in the homes of the pious Jews in the neighborhood. The pious Jew will not light a match on Saturday or on a religious holiday, or on the previous evening. At such times these women come to the house, light lamps for two cents, and start fires for five cents. They receive a dollar for a day's work.

They stand at their corners throughout the day, going from time to time to a Raines Law hotel or low saloon, where they drink ale and whiskey in the rear room. When one has had a couple of days' washing she must treat the crowd. Usually, however, when one has had that good fortune she drinks so much before she gets to her corner that she lands in the police station. The women live in garrets or cellars in Cherry Street, Mulberry Street, Baxter Street and Oliver Street, two or more occupying one room. Most of them are rounders or "revolvers"—that is, wretches who are repeatedly sent to the workhouse on the charge of drunk and disorderly.

There is comparatively little depravity and few criminals among the young—far less than might be expected in a city holding thousands of homeless gamins. This is in part due to the school attendance law, which compels parents and guardians to send children to school a certain number of weeks every year, and to the work of the Children's Aid Society, American Female Guardian Society, and the Society for the Prevention of Cruelty to Children. The Newsboys' lodging house has been a most potent factor in elevating the morals of the homeless little fellows. It has sheltered thousands who would otherwise have been driven to associate with the shiftless and vicious and in its way it has done more to prevent the production of criminals than any other institution or organization in the city.

There are some fellows who are instinctively vicious, who will not sell papers, black boots, or do any kind of work, but will steal, drink, smoke and associate with criminals.

They live under docks, or spend nights in club rooms, in cellars or in wagons. They are pickpockets or sneak thieves or aid the big "guns" or thieves in their projects and learn the tricks of their trade at so early an age that they become full-fledged crooks before they reach their teens.

They gamble, cheat, drink and comport themselves like old criminals, whose example they follow and whose ways they try to imitate.

Many of the young scamps live at home with vicious parents. In them depravity is inherited and developed by the example set before them. They are sent out to beg or steal, are praised when they are successful, and punished when they return empty-handed. These little fellows lead wretched lives, being on the street all day, often driven to desperation when they have been unsuccessful, fearing the beating at home yet more fearful of the dire punishment which, they had been told, would be inflicted if they fell into the hands of the police. Occasionally one will pluck up sufficient courage to say Gerry Society (Society for the Prevention of Cruelty to Children) at home. He is then beaten, starved and otherwise maltreated and made to swear that he will never repeat that name or attempt to inform that society. After he has been repeatedly beaten he will run away and the next few hours will decide his future career. He will not dare to tell his troubles to an officer unless hungry, and his usual recourse is to tell some newsboy, or ask him how to get some papers to sell. If he goes to the Newsboys' lodging house he is saved; otherwise he will steal and follow a criminal career.

There are some fellows who are bad in spite of good surroundings and moral teachings. These run away from home and join a gang, where they try to emulate the doings of the older boys. They follow the example of some tough and live like the homeless, vicious street gamins.

We read occasionally of schools where boys are taught to become pickpockets and sneak thieves. These are simply cases where the leader of the gang, generally the oldest fellow, shows the newcomer some tricks, and when the latter makes a haul the leader takes away the prize. When the novice is arrested he accuses the leader of having taught him the tricks and taking the proceeds of the thefts. The press then gives a sensational account of a "Fagin's" school for criminals.

CHAPTER VII

CRAFT AS A SCIENCE.

APPLIED to nobler purposes it would be called genius; as used by the beggar and criminal to obtain a livelihood without labor it is craft.

However repellant to the moral sense the methods may be, we must admire the successful beggar's keen discernment of character, the thief's daring and the trickster's knowledge of human nature.

The most successful of the beggars are the letter writers. They neither live nor work in Povertyville and may be dismissed with the remark, they are all frauds.

Street beggars depend either upon an infirmity to arouse sympathy, or upon appropriate pleas.

While there are many actual cripples among beggars, many are artificial cripples—"fake bandagers," they are called.

The hand strapped firmly to the shoulder with an artificial forearm, which can be rented by the day, makes an armless beggar. It is easier and more comfortable to strap the whole arm to the side, but this infirmity is looked upon with suspicion and an artificial arm is very expensive.

ROBBING A DRUNK.

It requires some acrobatic work to produce a one-legged beggar. The leg is strapped back upon the back of the thigh, and the imposter sits upon his foot; or the leg is stuck into an artificial leg, but such an appliance is expensive. One beggar was caught by the police after he had been at one place for months. He had one leg in a hole in a coal-hole cover, and had an artificial leg extended in its place. Blindness is simulated by folding the upper lids upwards—a simple trick—and turning the eyeballs upward. It is a difficult pose to maintain, but it produces a sympathy-arousing though repulsive appearance. Actual blindness may result from this. If the beggar wants to produce a woeful appearance without other infirmity he eats soap for a few days. His face becomes sallow and dark rings form under the eyes. These rings can be produced artificially. To these are added a hollow cough, a sad expression, tattered clothing which is several sizes too big for him, and the beggar appears to be in the last stages of consumption. His appearance arouses sympathy and he gets enough in a few days to recuperate for a month.

The most profitable form of deformity is the hunchback. This can be produced artificially by strapping a pad between the shoulder blades, raising the shoulders and allowing the head to sink into the characteristic position of the hunchback. It is only applicable to a small man.

THE WRETCHES

The hunchback stands at the entrance to pool rooms and race tracks and allows the sports to rub his back for a consideration. They think it is lucky to rub the hunch of a hunchback and pay for the privilege.

The beggar who does not depend upon infirmities, but relies upon appropriate pleas, is the artist of his calling.

He must understand human nature, must be able to read faces and must have a plausible excuse for his appeal, whatever form the plea may take. He will not accost a man in a hurry, for the latter will not stop to listen to him. Neither will he stop the man who walks along leisurely with coat buttoned up and hands in his pocket, looking about him, for that man is a sightseer who has heard of the wickedness of the Bowery and sees in any one who attempts to stop him a probable highwayman.

An appeal to a foreigner is wasted unless made in the foreigner's language.

The flashily-dressed man with a self-contented smile is probably a sport in luck and an appeal to him for the price of a drink will succeed, while an appeal for enough to pay for a night's lodging will fail. The same appeal works well with a lot of young men out for a good time, especially if one or two are already in a convivial humor.

The brawny westerner with wide-brimmed hat and open coat, who has come to see how bad the Bowery really is, is also the likely donor of the price of a drink.

When a man has had a drink or two he is in good humor and will listen to an appeal. The best time to strike him is on a Saturday night when he has his week's wages in his pocket. When he has had a few drinks he will be either liberal or combative. In either case the appeal for a drink will be more likely to succeed than any other.

The appeal for alms for a sick wife or child, or "just out of the hospital," or for a night's lodging does not work well with men on the Bowery. The sick wife story may work well with a man dressed in mourning and the "just out of the hospital" is usually given to elderly men. These or the appeal for enough to get a meal is usually tried on young couples. If they are not married the plea is usually successful, as the young man will then try to impress his companion with his generosity and good nature. If he is married he will show her that he is economical by refusing to give the beggar anything.

Women are more easily handled by beggars than men. The woman who is on her way to and from work, the woman with bundles in her arms and the woman in a hurry are avoided. If the beggar has a sickly appearance the most successful plea with women is for carfare to go to the hospital. Elderly women are easily impressed by the story of a sick mother, a starving family or "just out of the hospital," while the younger women respond more readily to a sick wife or children story. The night's lodging appeal works well in the evening when the beggar shows a probable donor that he has eight cents, and he needs two cents more to secure his bed. He generally gets a nickel and in the course of the evening may make half a dollar.

An appeal for food made by a fairly well-dressed individual is a profitable plea with women. The plea is seldom made to men unless it is genuine, as the man would take the beggar into a restaurant and pay for a meal.

There is one trick that is sure to elicit sympathy and nickels from women. The beggar rushes to the gutter or to a garbage pail, picks up a crust of bread and eats it as though he were starving. It is an old trick, but it works on passers-by, who are duped into giving the starving wretch enough to pay for several meals. When they are gone the crust goes back into the gutter, to be used a few moments later in the same manner when more women are approaching.

A plea which sometimes works with young women who want to be philanthropists but don't know how, is "just out of prison and no home to go to." The beggar making that plea ought to be, but rarely is, a convict or ex-convict. The real ex-convict who wishes to reform knows where he can obtain work and shelter and he will not depend upon begging.

Many tramps come to this city in the spring and fall and depend upon panhandling or begging on the streets. They trust to intimidation rather than to skillfully-worded appeals, and frequently fall afoul of the police.

THE WRETCHES

They will hold up individuals for the price of a drink or to "rush the growler," but they keep away from the Bowery district.

Female beggars are rare in Povertyville. A woman has so many resources from which she can obtain relief that she has no occasion to beg, and men have no sympathy with her.

Occasionally one will make a tour of the Bowery stores carrying a child, perhaps leading another, both hired for the purpose, but these wretches find a more fruitful field in the shopping district. Their usual plea is "a poor widow," a "sick husband," or "just out of the hospital."

There is a law against begging in the street. The professional beggar usually carries a bundle of pencils, ostensibly for sale, and thereby circumvents the law.

Those who beg by stopping individuals on the street and appealing directly to them use no subterfuge to violate the law. They do it openly, knowingly and willfully. If one of this class wears a soldier's uniform he is apparently free from arrest, unless he becomes drunk and disorderly. Others when caught are charged with vagrancy and go to Blackwell's Island.

There is little science employed by the petty criminals of Povertyville. There is often daring, some skill and some knowledge of human nature required in their work, but they are not confronted by the serious problems which the "big guns" or thieves are compelled to solve.

The meanest and lowest in the criminal social order is the "vogel grafter" or fellow who entices little children into hallways and robs them of their earnings, capes, coats, etc. He is but little worse than the thief who steals door mats and ash cans. Somewhat higher in the scale is the fellow who stops errand boys in the street, sends them on fictitious errands while he minds their parcels. When the errand boy returns the thief and parcel are gone.

More daring and skill are required by pickpockets. These generally work in "mobs" or gangs of three—two "stalls" and a "dip." One "stalls" in front and one behind the "sucker" or victim, while the "dip" makes the "touch" or theft. On car platforms the stalls stand at the side of the victim, the dip in front apparently reading a paper. Considerable skill is required to gently remove a man's watch from his pocket and twist it quickly off the ring. When the "dip" is ready to make the "touch" he gives a low, hoarse cough, or other signal. The others then stall—that is, they stand close to the victim and a little in front of him in such a way that he cannot move his arms forward; they then accidentally push him back. This attracts the victim's attention to the stall and away from the dip who had just jerked the watch from the chain. The "super" or watch is passed to a stall, who hurries away, while the "dip" continues on the car. No sign of recognition passes between the members of the mob when at work. A third stall is sometimes taken along to look out for the police, give the alarm and get in the way should the dip be chased. They call a detective a bull or an elbow and signal their companions that one is present by swinging an elbow forward or upward. This is a general sign, but mobs usually work out a system of signals among themselves.

The pickpocket has less difficulty with women, especially in a crowd. One of the stalls attracts a woman's attention, another stall pushes her from the opposite side and in the moment her attention is directed to the second stall, the dip has his hand in her hand satchel, extracting her pocketbook—"leather," they call it. When women wore large pockets in the side of their dresses pickpockets worked alone. Now women carry bags or satchels in front of them suspended from their wrists, and unless their attention is diverted for a moment by a stall they would notice the slight tug necessary to open the bag or satchel.

The pickpockets whose "graft" or dishonest work is to rob women are called "moll buzzers" or "moll wires." The dip is generally a youth in his teens. The stalls are older. When the dip becomes older and more ambitious he takes up the more hazardous work of lifting "supers" and pocketbooks from men. The Bowery furnishes most of the pickpockets, but they work principally in the shopping district, on the cars, at the bridge entrances and wherever crowds collect.

The sneak thief is also a product of Povertyville. He generally works alone, without a prearranged plan, and depends upon the opportunity to make a "touch." When engaged in "housework" (burglary) or "till tapping" (robbing money drawers) a pal or companion is necessary and plans must be made in advance. Either, however, can be done alone if the opportunity presents itself.

It is a poor and desperate criminal indeed who would attempt burglary in Povertyville. The prospective booty is slight, the danger of capture greater than if attempted in wealthier and less populous districts, and the punishment is as severe. (Burglary in criminal law is the breaking and entering a house with criminal intent at night. The same offense committed by day is larceny.)

The "house worker" works alone by day. He will go through a house pretending to be the directory man or a peddler of gas tips or some other small article that he can carry in his pocket. If he finds a door open and no one in the room he will take whatever he can lay his hands on. If a door is locked he looks through the keyhole to see if the room is occupied. A glance at the transom or hall window will give him the same information. A curtain over either window shows that it is not an empty apartment. With a pick lock he opens the door and can select the "swag" or booty at his leisure.

In a district where each house is occupied by one family he enters through the parlor window or, if a tenement is in the rear, he will go into the yard of the tenement, climb the fence and get into the yard of the house he intends to burglarize. On such expeditions he is usually accompanied by a pal, and has prearranged plans. By standing on his pal's shoulders he can reach the window of the back parlor, and from there he makes his way through the house. The pal at once returns to the tenement yard and hurries to the front of the house. The thief collects whatever of value he can find and goes out through the front door. When a big robbery in a private house is contemplated an accomplice in the house is desirable, even necessary.

This requires time, patience and money, and it is generally done by forming the acquaintance of one of the servants.

The girls are more gullible than the men, will listen to flattery, accept an invitation to go to a place of amusement followed by a dinner, and though it may take weeks or months, she will divulge the location of the jewel case, the precautions taken against burglars, the habits of the members of the family and the customary hours of dining and retiring. She may even consent to leave the front door open on the appointed evening, making the work of the thief simpler.

The sneak thieves of Povertyville have, however, neither the time, money, nor "nerve" to work such big game. More often they will bring a letter to the house and while the girl or butler carries the letter to the mistress of the house the thief will decamp with the coats and umbrellas on the hat rack, or some articles from the parlor. Another favorite game is to find out at what hour the master of the house usually returns from business, call at the house about half an hour before, present a card or letter and request that he be permitted to await the master's return. The request is usually granted but before the latter arrives the thief has departed with some articles of value. This trick is frequently practiced in physicians' offices, women as well as men working this easy graft.

Little craft, skill or courage is required in delivering fictitious telegrams or packages and collecting charges for the same. Notwithstanding the repeated exposé of this game it is one of the most successful of all dishonest ways of making money. A young man wearing a telegraph messenger's uniform delivers a telegram written upon the ordinary blank which anyone can obtain in the telegraph office, enclosed in an envelope similar to the regular envelopes in which messages are delivered. The charges written on the envelope are anywhere from twenty-five cents to a dollar. He collects the charges before delivering the envelope. The message may be some ironical remark about the recipient's gullibility. Packages containing sawdust or bricks are delivered in the same way, the person delivering the package wearing the uniform of a telegraph messenger or expressman. A trick which is very successful around the Christmas holidays is worked as follows: A few minutes after the delivery wagon of a department store has delivered a parcel at a residence an expressman enters with another parcel, states that the one just delivered was wrongly addressed and he had the one which belonged there. He departs with the parcel first delivered and leaves his own, which contains sawdust or rags.

Many physicians have been victims of the following trick: The physician is called to a patient some distance from his office. Soon after the doctor has left the office the messenger who had called for him returns and tells the person at the door that the doctor had sent him back for his instrument satchel. The messenger receives it and hurries away. The doctor returns from a wild goose chase and learns that his instruments are gone.

Till-tapping has become unprofitable since the introduction of the cash register, still it is occasionally practiced in stores where there is no such safeguard.

In bakeries, groceries and butcher shops where the principal business is done in the morning, the noon hour is selected; in other stores, before closing.

A stall engages the proprietor in conversation and manages to get him out of the store or in a corner. By pretending to be the building inspector and showing a badge the stall has an opportunity to go into the cellar, and call the proprietor out of the store to accompany him. The tapper, usually a boy, sneaks in, gets behind a counter, opens the till, takes all the bills he can grasp, and runs out; if there is an open rear window or side door he goes out that way. If the proprietor "gets wise" or finds out that he is being robbed, the stall "slugs" or hits him on the head and runs away.

Shoplifting is the female criminal's special graft, although many of Povertyville's sneak thieves work it. It requires little skill or daring and the men who work it are considered among the "cheap guns" or petty thieves. Some female shoplifters are skillful in secreting the plunder and audacious in their work. They invariably wear a long cloak or coat under which the stuff is hidden. When one wears a cloak she sews a few hooks on the inside or has pockets in it into which the things are dropped. One hook is sewed inside near the edge, and while standing near the counter she dextrously fastens some article to the hook and, partly turning, the article is swept inside the cloak, her hands being exposed. When she leaves the counter the stolen article goes into a pocket or on another hook. Shoplifters who work in the shopping districts work alone, preferably at the bargain counters. The high-class shoplifters who work jewelry, silk and fur stores, and these departments in the department stores, work in pairs. They dress well, act well and make a good appearance, frequently come in a carriage and make a great display of money. They do not live or work in Povertyville.

Most of the "shovers of the queer," or passers of counterfeit money, are residents of Povertyville.

Nearly all the counterfeit coin is handled by Italians, who pass it singly in small trade in which they receive change. There is little business done in selling counterfeit coin in bulk. Much is passed upon hucksters and store keepers, but little goes over the saloon bars. Nor is there any trade in counterfeit bills in Povertyville. What counterfeit bills come into the district are brought in accidentally by persons ignorant of the fact until apprised thereof. Such bills are generally passed in saloons. Bartenders will sometimes accept a counterfeit bill at a discount, pocketing the difference. The bill is placed in the drawer, and is either passed in the course of business or given to the beer collector.

The more ambitious criminals, burglars, forgers, and what are known as "big guns" or "number one men," do not work or live in Povertyville, but there are many "crooks" or professional rogues in the district.

It is impossible to name all the tricks of the wretches who live by craft. New tricks are worked and new games are played every day by men who live by their wits; many are ingenious, some within the letter of the law, yet as fraudulent as forgery. Some old games have been given a world-wide publicity, yet find victims in credulous farmers and rural merchants, while new variations are often successfully worked upon "wise" city folks.

The gold brick game, one of the most profitable swindles known, has been worked ever since the California gold miners returned to New York with lumps of gold in the early fifties. The swindler procures a brick or cone of brass, it is thinly plated with gold to withstand the acid test, and then two or three borings made which are then filled with gold. A "sucker" or victim is found who is willing to buy a brick of gold "dropped from the wagon going to the mint." The brick is worth $2,000, but Mr. Jay can have it for $500. An accomplice has an office with the word "assayer" on the door. The seller and the victim go to the assayer, who removes one of the gold plugs and pronounces it pure gold. Another plug is removed and taken to another assayer, a reputable one this time, and this is pronounced genuine. The deal is consummated in the office of the pretended assayer. Mr. Jay departs, and the swindler has disposed of a fifteen-dollar brick containing ten dollars gold for five hundred dollars. This game works better in the west than in New York, where it has been overdone.

The green goods swindle is still worked successfully, although it has been repeatedly exposed. The green goods men send out a large number of letters equivocally worded, but leaving no doubt that a deal in counterfeit money is intended, although neither the word money nor dollars is mentioned. These letters are sent to farmers and country merchants. To those who send a favorable reply, they send a second letter, sometimes enclosing half of a new one dollar bill, and offer a thousand like sample for three hundred, five thousand for seven hundred, ten thousand for a thousand. The "Jay," "Rube" or "Yap," as the victim is called, has been known to send the cash without further inquiry. Of course, he never hears from his correspondents again. As a rule, however, he is invited to come to the city, and meet his friends at some hotel. He is given explicit directions how to bring the money, what name to assume, what train to take, and how he will be able to recognize the one who is to meet him at the depot. The farmer follows the directions, is taken to the dealer's room, and is shown a bundle of good money and many similar bundles in a trunk. He buys a "1,000 for 300," "5,000 for 700," or "10,000 for 1,000," the bundles are placed in the farmer's valise or bag, and he departs. At home he finds the bottom and top bills are genuine, the rest is stage money. He has been participating in a criminal transaction, and has no redress. A variation of the game is to place genuine money in the satchel in the victim's presence, and while his attention is diverted for a moment a dummy satchel is put in the place of the other.

Any game by which a person is swindled is really a bunco game. Usually the name is applied to a scheme by which a stranger is lured into a house by a decoy and there fleeced by the confederate.

Mr. Jay may be accosted on the street by a stranger who asks him the direction to some street. Mr. Jay shows by his ignorance that he is a stranger in the city, and Mr. Bunco Steerer finds an excuse for continuing the conversation, learns where he is from and where he is stopping. If Mr. Jay is loquacious he will give his name and the business that has brought him here. If he has been simple enough to give the steerer this information he may learn that the gentleman he is talking to is the president of the bank in the next town, or that his new acquaintance is here on an errand similar to his own. More often after Mr. Steerer has learned Mr. Jay's name he will leave him, and a few minutes later Mr. Jay will be hailed by someone who knows his name and comes from an adjoining village. A stranger in a great city is always glad to meet someone from his own neighborhood, and Mr. Jay is no exception. He will accept his neighbor's invitation to drink, and go to his room or go to his hotel. There he is interested in a game of cards or in a dispute in which bets are made. Mr. Jay bets or lends money to his newly-found friend to bet, or will cash a check for him, or they may go into the next room where a party is playing cards and he is induced to join the game.

The friend will win with ridiculous ease, and Mr. Jay will try his hand. He will win a little, but the stakes will suddenly be raised and Mr. Jay loses all he has.

A more successful method to gain the victim's confidence after it is found that he is a stranger in the city, is to follow him to his hotel and there learn his name from the hotel register. This requires some diplomacy.

The steerer may find it necessary to hire a room in the hotel to learn what room Mr. Jay occupies, then from the hotel register learn the name and residence of the occupant. Mr. Jay receives a letter from the "nephew of the president of the bank" in Mr. Jay's town, inviting him to call. The nephew has heard from his uncle that Mr. Jay was in town, and wants to warn him against green goods men and bunco steerers. Mr. Jay tells the nephew what brought him here. Then the confederate enters, representing himself as a lawyer, stock broker, ranch owner, or any character the occasion may require. In whatever line the victim may be interested and most likely to invest money the confederate is similarly interested. Mr. Jay may take up a mortgage on a farm which has no existence, or buy cattle to be delivered in a week, or a threshing machine selected from an agricultural catalogue at half price, to be shipped from the factory, or he may buy worthless mining stock. Mr. Jay may even conspire with the nephew to beat the imaginary uncle. The nephew buys for his uncle valuable stock much below market price and Mr. Jay is to deliver the stock to the uncle and receive from him the full price. Mr. Jay must leave a deposit and send the nephew half of the profit. When Mr. Jay returns home he finds that the bank president has no nephew in New York, the stock is worthless, his purchases do not arrive, and he has been buncoed.

There are many variations of this game. The simplest form is to inveigle Mr. Jay into a game of cards with a stranger, Mr. Nephew promising to make good any loss Mr. Jay may have. Mr. Nephew makes good with a bad check.

A novel swindle has recently been tried with success. Mr. Jay is asked to sign a petition to the legislature to reduce railroad fares. The petition is filled with names and only one space is left in which he signs his own. The blank space is prepared by cutting out a piece of the fictitious petition and passing underneath a blank note or check. Mr. Jay signs his name in the blank space, believing he has signed the petition. Mr. Jay recently lost his trunk in a hotel in this city by this trick. He had in some (to him) unaccountable way signed his name to a sheet of hotel stationery. The order for his trunk was filled in over his signature.

Since the Tenderloin has become the sight-seeing district of this city, bunco games are seldom worked on the Bowery. The son of Mr. Jay's old friend and the nephew of the president of the bank find their dupes most frequently on Broadway and near the ferries, just as credulous, greedy and gullible as ever.

The real mock auction of the Bowery is a thing of the past.

Before stringent laws were made defining the auctioneer's duties and liabilities and fixing a high license fee, a mock auctioneer would hire a store for a day or two, fill it with all sorts of trash and auction it off. Cappers would bid up the prices and when a few sales were made at high prices the place would close.

Plated watches, jewelry, tableware and paste gems were most frequently disposed of.

The cheapest watches, having, however, the name of a noted maker on the dial plate, in plated cases, were sold as genuine Howards, Jurgensens, etc., in solid gold cases.

Where a place was rented for a week or a month a large stock was put in, and after an auctioneer had made a fraudulent sale, he disappeared and one of the cappers would take his place. Cigars were sold in the same manner. The auctioneer would tell buyers they were smuggled and must be sold quickly before government officers could locate them. One would be pushed out of a bundle and given to a prospective purchaser. The latter would try it, find it good, and purchase the bundle. The cigars with the exception of the sample, were the vilest imaginable.

Mock auction sales of cigars and trash are still conducted, but keep within the letter of the law. An accomplice of the auctioneer hires a store, fills it with cheap cigars or cheap stuff intended for the sale. He does a legitimate business for a few days, then the place is sold at auction. The sale itself is honestly conducted, as the auctioneer will not jeopardize his $2,000 bond by making misrepresentations. Whatever deception is practiced is in what is left unsaid. The presence of cappers who bid up goods, but never buy, determines the character of the sale.

The bunco schemes requiring a large amount of money to begin with, like the green goods game, or requiring specially prepared rooms or apartments, like the panel game and wire tapping game, are no longer profitable on the Bowery, still "suckers" are occasionally caught there while sightseeing. The neighborhood of the Bowery was once a fruitful field in which to work the panel game. The victim would visit a house of ill fame and place his clothes and satchel on a chair or trunk near the wall. A hole in the wall was covered by a picture or lithograph, and through it the victim's clothes and satchel were drawn, rifled and returned. Men carrying much money do not visit such houses in Povertyville now. In the wire tapping game the victim is told that the telegraph wire leading to a pool room has been secretly tapped, and information from the race track is received in time to lay wagers in the pool room after a race has been run. A telegraph receiver is placed in the room and a wire leading to it comes in at the window. The receiver is, however, connected with a push button under the edge of the table and is worked by a confederate, while another confederate is waiting on the street, ostensibly to run to the pool room as soon as he receives signals previously arranged between him, the wire tapper and the victim. When all is ready the pseudo-telegraph operator reads the returns from the receiver, the victim is induced to make a large bet quickly, paying the money to the two men in the room. The confederate on the street receives the signal and runs off. The telegraph operator goes out to fix the wire, and when he fails to return the other one goes after him. When the victim is tired of waiting, he realizes that a "sucker is born every minute." The badger game, though extensively worked, does not pay on the Bowery. It is simply a form of blackmail. A man accepts a woman's invitation to visit her in her house, and when they are in a compromising position the "injured husband" enters. The victim will give all he has about him to get out of the scrape. A man who has a reputation to uphold will stand considerable loss rather than exposure, but if he understands the game and retains his presence of mind, he will defy them.

If the couple working this game know that the victim is a man of prominence they work it differently. She gets the victim in such a position that a photograph can be taken of him in the compromising position. The photograph is taken over the transom or through a panel, and the negative becomes a permanent source of income.

Such photographs and compromising letters are the principal tools of the blackmailers.

Blackmailing is a lost art in Povertyville since the rich men, those who can stand the constant drain, no longer go there for their pleasures and do not become involved with its comparatively plain, poorly dressed wretches.

Of the many small schemes practiced in Povertyville to fleece the unwary, flim-flam is the most prevalent. This is a sleight-of-hand trick in making change, by which a waiter will extract a bill after the change has been counted to the victim, or he may fold a bill in half and count the two ends. It cannot succeed, if one will count the bills after receiving them from the waiter, but the latter has a way of disappearing immediately after he has given a customer short change.

If the person has given the waiter a large bill, the waiter counts the change in the patron's presence, then extracts the bottom bill as he hands it over. If the victim finds he is flim-flammed and complains, the waiter will again take the money, count it, make good the deficiency, and in returning it will again extract the bottom bill. Having seen the waiter return the bill, the patron is generally satisfied and puts the change in his pocket without recounting it. This occurs so often that the flim-flammer invariably places a one dollar bill at the bottom and a larger bill next to it, to be withdrawn when the change is returned the second time. One should never give a large bill, but having done so he should not return the change to his pocket until he has counted it.

The soap game is usually worked on the Bowery corners. A fakir has a satchel containing a number of small boxes, each holding a cake of soap. When he has collected a crowd he places a ten dollar bill in one of the boxes, throws it conspicuously on the top of the heap, and allows anyone to pick out three boxes for five dollars. A capper or confederate buys three boxes, including the one containing the bill, shows it to the bystanders and walks away. The operation is repeated, and a "sucker" picks out three boxes, including the one he supposes contains the bill. The fakir had, however, palmed that box and dropped an empty one in its place. Sometimes he will place old green beer barrel revenue stamps in a few boxes, and leave a small corner of the stamp exposed when the box is closed. The box containing the genuine bill never leaves his hand except when the capper buys it. The three card monte men and the shell men have been driven off the street, but they occasionally find victims in its saloons. Both depend upon sleight-of-hand tricks to beat the unwary bettor. The monte man shows three cards, one a court card, throws them on a table face downward, and bets that the victim cannot pick out the court card. A capper holds the stakes. The bettor rarely succeeds in picking out the right card, but if he does he finds that the stakeholder has disappeared.

The shell game is similar. The manipulator uses three walnut shells and a pea which he rolls from one shell to the other. He then bets a bystander that the latter does not know under which shell the pea is. The honest shell man takes chances, the odds being two to one in his favor. The dishonest shell man takes no chances. The pea sticks to his finger when it stops rolling, and is supposed to be under the shell.

A little sympathy might be bestowed upon the credulous simpleton who is taken in by the bunco man's plausible tale, but the fool who plays cards or dice with a stranger deserves none.

There are innumerable ways by which the professional gambler can cheat at cards. With a novice he will depend upon his skill in shuffling and dealing, and so expert do some gamblers become that they can deal any hand they wish. When they play with more experienced players who know a trick or two about stacking cards and crooked dealing they depend upon marked cards. In these there is some peculiarity in the device on the back by which they can tell the face. The ordinary marked cards sold by dealers have a line thickened or a dot misplaced, the position indicating the face. These are well known to professional players, and the dishonest gambler will use an honest deck to which he will add the marks himself.

It matters not what game the novice plays with the professional gambler, he will be fleeced. He has some chance in a gambling house in games where paraphernalia is used, and the house is satisfied with the ordinary percentage which falls to it. There are, however, crooked apparatus by which the percentage in favor of the house can be enormously increased.

THE WRETCHES

When the city is run open and gambling houses spring up all over town, those on the Bowery use these crooked appliances. At present, when the few gambling houses in the district are run as clubs, and none but the members can enter, the games are run straight, and the novice, if he can get in, stands some chance for his money.

There are tricks in dice-throwing by which the uninitiated can be as readily fleeced as with cards. There are two forms of crooked dice, loaded and shaped, the former heavier on one side, the latter slightly rounded on one or more sides. An expert can manipulate such dice with sufficient dexterity to overcome the weight and shape.

Where the stakes are big sleight-of-hand tricks are tried, the victim using dice loaded or shaped to throw low, his opponent using dice shaped or loaded to throw high. Even wise city folks are sometimes inveigled into buying articles which the "con" (confidence man) has just picked up. As the victim walks along he sees a man crossing the street, then suddenly stooping, pick up from the gutter a diamond ring. The man offers to sell the ring to the victim, telling him that as he must leave the city he cannot wait for the reward which will certainly be offered for its return. All the victim pays over five cents is clear gain for the "con," who had placed the ring in the gutter. The operator may pick up a well-filled pocketbook or a wallet, and show that it contains a roll of bills. On the same plea, that of leaving the city, he disposes of his find. The outside bill is a genuine one dollar bill, the rest is green paper. Mr. "Con" may offer to sell a gold watch which he says he had just "swiped." The stranger who may pay five dollars for what appears to be worth ten times that amount, finds out too late that the watch is plated, and costs sixty cents.

Notwithstanding the repeated exposes of the tricks and games practiced by bunco men and gamblers, they find victims continually, using the same old methods which caught the fathers and grandfathers of the present generation. But new games are devised every day, and it is only by suspecting the motive of every stranger who wishes to befriend, by refusing to be inveigled into any scheme or game, by declining to buy anything unless one knows the actual value of his purchase and receives it before he shows his money, that one is safe from craft and fraud.

CHAPTER VIII

SIDE LIGHTS.

THE wretches of Povertyville who were accustomed to good clothes and clean surroundings retain a sense of neatness until they part with their last white shirt. Even then some try to retain an air of respectability, and by begging or borrowing obtain enough money to buy a rubber or celluloid shirt front, collar and cuffs, using the strips of their last white shirt for ties.

Some become quite expert with the needle and can hem edges as neatly as a seamstress. They repair their clothing, sew up rips and tears, put on patches, let out seams and make alterations that lie within the province of the tailor. Shakespeare might have had such as these in mind when he wrote, "One touch of nature makes the whole world kin," for here we find the man who could wield the pen, handle a yacht or build an engine, become equally expert with the needle and thread. One touch of poverty makes tailors of them all.

How to obtain clothing is one of the serious problems which confront the penniless yet fastidious wretch. As he cannot afford to buy new clothes he must fall back upon second-hand, refurbished wearing apparel. A new (second-hand) hat costs from fifteen to fifty cents, but the hat racks in the restaurants generally furnish a choice selection. The exchange of hats in the restaurants and barber shops is a common mode of obtaining better headgear. Strips of muslin or flannel wrapped around the feet form a substitute for socks, but nothing can take the place of shoes. These are heeled, soled, patched and sewed as long as sole and upper will hold together. When the wretch is in luck he will buy a second-hand pair in the "Bay" (Baxter Street) for fifty cents. The dealer charges a dollar, the wretch offers a quarter and they compromise on fifty cents. That is the usual price and the usual method of dealing, although poor fits, odd sizes and other flaws reduce the price.

When he cannot afford to buy a pair he will have a patch nailed over the hole in the sole for ten cents, or new heels put on for fifteen cents. When the sole and vamp threaten to part company the cobbler hammers in a few nails and harmony is restored at the small cost of five cents. To mend a tear which needle and thread can repair costs nothing—the wretch does that himself. The simplest way to obtain clothing is to beg for cast-off clothing from a charitable society. There are several which collect and distribute clothing, but most of them require references. The poor devil who has had the foresight to attend mission meetings frequently will be known to the conductor of the mission and can then use him as reference.

If he can afford to spend a dollar or two he will go to the Bay and buy a good suit, one that has been re-dyed and altered so that the original owner cannot recognize it. Much cast-off clothing and most of the clothing which leaves the owner without his knowledge or consent find their way into the Bay. Overcoats cost from fifty cents to a dollar; underwear, ten to twenty-five cents.

Laundry work is another serious problem with fastidious fellows. Some reserve their only white shirt for special occasions. The celluloid or rubber collars, cuffs, and shirt fronts require only the application of a damp cloth to restore their gloss and whiteness.

Underwear, however, must be washed occasionally and many do that work themselves. Some lodging houses have drying rooms where the lodgers can wash and dry their clothes. If the poor devil is stopping at a lodging house which has not these conveniences he does his laundry work in his wash basin. He soaks the underwear in hot water for a few minutes, rubs them with soap, rinses them a few times in cold water, wrings them out with his hands and hangs them around the steam pipe, heater or stove. This is done at night and in the morning they are dry. To straighten out the folds and wrinkles the wash is placed between the sheet and mattress for an hour, during which he occupies the bed. Necessity is the mother of invention.

The female wretches of Povertyville have little difficulty in replenishing their wardrobes. They depend mainly upon the generosity of their lovers, but for expensive finery they go to the department stores and help themselves when the watchers are not looking. As the well-dressed women are more successful in their vocation than the shabbily-dressed ones, outer garments are part of their trade stock. Their dresses are cast-off or stolen and altered, and obtained either directly from a fence or from a second-hand clothing store.

The wretches are charitable among themselves and help each other in adversity, but they rarely apply to charities. As a last resort they go to the Salvation Army.

The ordinary women of the street are careless about their wardrobe except the outer wear. Cloaks, waists and skirts are mended, but other wearing apparel is allowed to become rags, pinned together. They are cleanly about their persons but indifferent about their surroundings. They will not sweep their rooms, clean windows, nor make up beds except in a slipshod manner, nor will they do anything requiring physical exertion which can be left undone. Their moral and their æsthetic sense are on a par. When they reach that stage where they can no longer attract a patron, they become indifferent to their appearance and person, going in rags until supplied with new clothing in the workhouse. It may be mentioned incidentally that clothes and shoes are repaired in the prison shops.

The petty criminals of Povertyville steal what they need either from stores or from drunks. There is no charity in that class and they will not help out a friend in need. What they do not require for their own use goes to a fence. They despise a "sucker," or one who will allow himself to be robbed or beaten in a game, and they place themselves in the same category if anyone gets something for nothing from them.

The wretches of Povertyville have few amusements. Having little need for mental or physical recreation, they become apathetic, exercise is irksome and they drift along, neither needing nor seeking change from their accustomed routine.

They take little interest in the passing events of the day and only some event of extraordinary interest or involving their own welfare will arouse them. Their main pastime is gambling and this applies to all classes except those far gone as drunks and pipe fiends. These find recreation, pleasure, excitement and consolation in the whiskey glass or pipe. The men who can afford it go to the pool rooms and gambling houses or play poker in their rooms. The inmates of the poor lodging houses, the beggars and tramps play cards or throw dice in their lodging houses or in saloons. Games requiring mental effort are rarely taken up. Occasionally two men will play checkers in the sitting room of a lodging house, a checker board being marked off on a table with chalk, and black and white buttons serving for pieces.

Backgammon is sometimes played when a board can be obtained, but dice are always at hand and crap shooting is very common. The possessor of a deck of cards is never without a companion in a lodging house. The cards are often so disfigured from frequent handling that every card is recognizable from marks on the back, and missing cards are replaced by pieces of card board cut the same size as the cards, but these disadvantages are not taken into account. When the players can get two decks pinochle is the favorite game; with one deck poker is the prime favorite. The nominal stakes are high, but the final settlement is so small that the player who has lost hundreds of dollars pays in fact but a few cents. Next to poker come euchre, Sancho Pedro and cribbage.

In the clubs where the wretches who allow dissolute women to support them congregate, poker is the usual game and a single "pot" may hold the earnings of several women for days. The professional gamblers, and sports and criminals when in luck, play in the gambling houses and stick to faro and roulette. It is strange that the gambler should prefer to play roulette, which, even when honestly conducted, gives a decided percentage in favor of the house, rather than games giving equal chances. Policy was formerly *the* game of Povertyville, and many a too-confident votary of the horse, gig, saddle and cap in policy has thereby been driven to join the army of wretches. The active work of the anti-policy society in New York has almost entirely eradicated this evil and has prevented untold misery and wretchedness in poor homes. The wretches who formerly played policy now play other games, but the wives and children of the workingmen in the tenement districts, who formerly stinted themselves for clothes and food in order to buy the deceptive slips, now buy instead the necessities of life.

Many in whom the gambling habit has not been entirely squashed by the exposure of the policy fraud now buy lottery tickets. There is still some policy played in the city, but policy shops in Povertyville have been closed and those who still believe they can beat the game get their slips from a runner or agent who meets his victims in a cigar store in the morning and reports the winning numbers in the same place in the afternoon.

Old-time sports occasionally look at the sporting bulletins posted in saloons and discuss the merits of the contestants in coming sporting events, but unless they can bet they prefer reminiscences to prognostications.

Many spend their days in reading rooms and their evenings in missions and lecture halls when it is cold or stormy. In pleasant weather they lounge about on park benches. A few, and these almost without exception exotics, go to the reading rooms for mental recreation.

The female wretches have few amusements. They sometimes play pinochle, casino, euchre or poker with their lovers, and occasionally take part in a dance at a dive. When they go to a theater it is to find likely patrons. The only amusement not lessened by the hunt for customers is the annual ball of the club to which the lover belongs.

During the progress of a ball given by one of the clubs in the Bowery district the dives are comparatively empty and the street is bare of women of this class.

A strange trait in the character of the wretches, even of the most vicious and callous, is a deep sense of humanity which they occasionally exhibit. The thug who would not hesitate to assault a police officer or rob a child will let a priest pass without molestation. A physician carrying a satchel, on his way to a patient, is perfectly safe among a gang of cutthroats as soon as they know his vocation. The "vogel grafter" or robber of little children has some standing among his class, but let him assault or hurt a child and his best friend would turn against him. They have little respect for women and show little consideraion for the aged, but they will shield and protect the young. When they find a boy with vicious proclivities they will endeavor to develop them, but they will not attempt to instil viciousness into a boy who is naturally good.

Most sneak thieves and burglars are superstitious and have a fear of robbing a church. Not one would rob a church of his own denomination. While irreligious, when they think they are about to die they call for a priest or minister. At all other times they reject religious teachings altogether or receive them with the idea that it may come in handy in their work.

Some of the women go to church and are there quite devout, but their idea of the golden rule is, "Do others lest others do you."

Heroic actions performed by wretches are not rare. They exhibit that form of heroism which springs up suddenly in an emergency and takes no cognizance of personal danger.

Few of the wretches possess that courage which is required when the danger to be encountered is known and appreciated in advance. Some do perform foolhardy acts to gain notoriety, while many of the sports will not shrink from fist fights with more powerful men to gain a standing. Desperation nerves the criminal to attack a police officer in his efforts to escape arrest, but the young tough will try to "do the cop" in a spirit of bravado. If he succeeds he is the hero of his class.

Some classes among the wretches seek to attract attention to themselves, others try to avoid it. The sport wears a loud checked suit of clothes, the bunco man makes a display of jewelry and money. The pickpocket wears while at work good clothes but inconspicuous colors. The sneak thief is generally shabbily dressed, although he may have a hundred dollars or more with him to be used as "fall money" or money to be paid to a lawyer or for bail in case of his arrest.

THE WRETCHES

The women of the street wear bright colors, while the shoplifter is most successful when dressed in mourning or subdued colors. The poor devil has little choice in the matter of dress, but prefers such colors as show dust and wear least.

The wretches, with the exception of tramps and sots, keep their faces in presentable condition. Those who cannot afford the price of a shave (five cents in many shops) go to a barber school where they are shaved free by pupils. Old professional beggars use a chemical, aurum pigment, which they mix with water, forming a paste, and rub this on their faces. In a few moments this is scraped off with a piece of wood. The chemical burns off the hair without affecting the skin. The others, when they can afford the price of a shave, go to one of the thirty-five barber shops on the street, but haircutting is generally done by a friend in the lodging house or by a pupil of the barber school.

Gamblers, sports and the female wretches almost without exception are superstitious and carry talismans, usually a "luck penny," a cent of the date of the person's birth. They will rub the hump of a hunchback for luck, but if a cross-eyed person enters the room they will leave it, or if they must remain they will keep their fingers crossed. Everyone has some secret formula which is repeated when a cross-eyed person passes them, if they see a funeral approaching or if they are obliged to pass between two funeral carriages. They have dream and omen books, which are consulted on every possible occasion, and while they will not go to a fortune teller—as they fear the latter might make some frightful prophecy—they have unbounded faith in their printed oracle. There is little social intercourse among the poor devils in the lodging houses. Gamblers and sports have many acquaintances, but few friends and no intimates. Criminals, on the other hand, have many friends and nearly every one has his pals or intimate co-workers. The women, as a rule, have intimate female friends to whom they confide everything except the history of their lives before their downfall. They are rarely sincere, however, and not one would make any sacrifice for another. While charitable, as a rule, they would do nothing for another which might endanger their own safety or freedom. The relationship between the women and their lovers is peculiar. There is no love or affection on either side—nothing but a business interest. She is the earner, he is her protector. For such protection she gives him all she earns; having once accepted him as her lover she submits to his wishes, and the harsher he thereafter treats her the more slavishly will she follow him. When he is tired of her he turns her adrift.

The relationship between the criminals and their mistresses is more conjugal. There is generally love and affection—always jealousy. He may have taken her from the street, but from the moment he makes her his "Moll" she must be faithful to him. In adversity he may send her out on the street to help support the household, but unless they follow the blackmailing or badger game he expects her to abide by the same code of ethics as if they were married. If he treats her harshly she leaves him, while he, on the other hand, turns her adrift if he suspects that she has been intimate with another unless with his consent. This peculiar marital or conjugal relationship is not based upon any sense of morality or propriety, but upon selfishness. They do not respect the honor of woman, for chastity is, in their opinion, not due to any moral sense, but to the fear of consequences. The affection between the criminal and his mistress is more of a Platonic nature, their sexual relations being of minor consideration. At the same time he will not permit her to dispense her favors to another unless business is bad, when he will send her on the street to pick up customers. On rare occasions he will lend her to a friend or exchange "Molls" with a pal. If he is sent to prison she will associate with another criminal, and upon the release of her former companion she will decide with which one she will remain. Where two or three couple occupy a flat together they form a free-love community in their sexual and housekeeping relations. In other respects each couple looks after its own affairs. They never marry.

CHAPTER IX

THE FINAL ACCOUNTING.

FEW notice their coming, fewer still their passing away.

The "rounders," "floaters," "revolvers," as they are called, are not missed, although they may have been patrons at the same bar and in the same lodging house for years.

Out of sight they are forgotten—their places are taken up by new recruits who follow in their footsteps.

Most disappear as mysteriously as they came, a few are last seen in a police patrol wagon or in an ambulance, a few turn up again a few years later regenerated, visitors to the haunts which sheltered them in darker days.

Few end their career by their own hands—"do the Dutch act," as they call suicide. It is only in the early stages when the wretch has still some sense of honor and shame, some realization of his degradation, and some regard for his family, that remorse may drive him to end it all. But he has still hope left—a hope that something will turn up to better his position. When hope has fled he no longer cares how long or how short may be his span of life. He has then neither energy nor ambition. So valueless does life appear to him that he would not stir to save it, or do aught to end it; the fear of physical pain deters him from the latter course and rouses him when danger threatens. He would lie upon the floor awaiting death did not the pangs of hunger and thirst drive him out.

While life has no attraction and death no horror, yet he dreads the momentary pang with which he believes death is associated. This wretch never commits suicide.

Almost all the wretches who go down through drink end their days in the wards of Bellevue or the Penitentiary Hospital. Either Bright's disease or cirrhosis of the liver carries them off.

Occasionally one is found dead in his bed or on the street, or too ill to work, is carried to the police station, put in a cell, "drunk" marked next to his name on the blotter and "dead" a few hours later.

A frequent cause of death is the sudden and complete deprivation of drink after a long debauch. The wretch then sees things—not snakes, as the popular impression is, but horrible forms, devils, wolves, headless bodies—a frightful phantasmagoria from which he tries to escape. It is delirium tremens, the D. T. of the hospital record, which ends in a stupor, followed by death. The D. T. cases go to the alcoholic ward of Bellevue Hospital, the Bright's disease and cirrhosis cases are usually transferred to the City Hospital. This is the material which is furnished to the dissecting rooms of the medical colleges.

THE WRETCHES

A patient entering the hospital gives the name of a friend who is to be informed "if anything happens." The wretches have no friends and when they die there are none to mourn their loss; living unrespected, they die unregretted.

Occasionally, however, when a wretch realizes that the end is near, he will give the name of one who is near and dear to him, and whose name he has saved from disgrace. When all is over he is quietly removed to the family vault.

Some wretches are reclaimed and reform. This can be done through the power of prayer backed with the opportunity and means to remain reformed. The prayer is like the varnish on the post. It improves the appearance, but it is the backing and not the gloss which keeps the wretch up.

The young man fresh from the country and home influences, perhaps still carrying the little Bible his mother gave him, is susceptible to the influence of prayer until his last nickel is gone. After that, the solid backing will be necessary to sustain him. Prayer no longer will have any power to keep him in the straight and narrow path.

When the hardened wretch professes conversion he does so with some mental reservation and an ulterior motive. He is never sincere.

Sometimes a passing incident in the wretch's life will swerve him from his course. The sight of the dying agony of one who was run over on the Bowery while drunk, sobered his companion and reformed him. Another was recognized by a former college chum who was on a slumming expedition. The chum found the wretch the next night in a groggery and took him in a carriage to his own home. A compulsory bath, clean clothing, a good room and meals, and constant watching made a man of the wretch in a month.

One reformed thief ascribes his reformation to a dream the nature of which he will not divulge. Another pickpocket was reformed through the tact of a woman he had robbed.

She offered a reward for papers which were in a purse he had picked, and when he came to return the papers she had a lengthy conversation with him. She offered him work and a substantial reward if he would serve faithfully for a year, which offer he accepted. There was no word about morals at the time, but before the year was up he had become a church member and has since reformed many wretches by methods similar to those employed by his patroness.

The Salvation Army and the Volunteers of America have reclaimed many wretches, some by moral persuasion alone, others by aid when the wretches came to them in distress.

A few have reformed after a short time in prison, The deterrent effect of the punishment, the sense of degradation produced, and later the helping hand of the

Prison Association placing them in a position where they could earn a livelihood away from evil influences and rehabilitate themselves, have restored some to respectability.

Lengthy association with the vicious and criminal in prison destroys whatever sense of honor and shame a man may have left when entering jail. Upon his release he is a hardened and confirmed criminal.

Most wretches reform when they are, or believe they are, on their deathbed, but if they recover they are backsliders. The widower, drinking himself to death to forget his sorrows, goes down as a sot. So, too, the man deserted by his wife, while if he is the deserter moral influence may recall him; force, never.

The male wretches never marry unless they reform. The criminals live with their female companions without any regard for marriage ceremonies or their own legal status. They demand, however, that the woman remain faithful while the co-partnership lasts. Those who live on the earnings of the women of the street do not marry them.

One case, however, is known where such a woman reformed, succeeded in reforming her lover, then marrying him. They are now doing missionary work in Povertyville, following the practical method of handling individual cases only; not hopeless sots or hardened criminals, but newcomers.

The old female rounders end their days as the same class of men, Bright's disease or cirrhosis carrying them off; they rarely get delirium tremens. They drop off in alleyways or gutters or in the wards of the Bellevue, City or Penitentiary hospitals.

Among the younger female wretches a few reform, many drift along for a few years, become ill and die in the hospital, some become criminals or keepers of houses of ill fame, a few become sots. The gay and giddy take up opium smoking with its fearful end. This class never reform. Towards the end one may become the "wife" of a Chinaman, who will look after her welfare, but her end is the same as the usual end of male smokers—consumption. Or one who has not yet become a confirmed smoker, and while she can still overcome the "yin," may, under stress of circumstances, go to a home or reformatory, but the old life is too attractive. She goes back to the whirl, to the pipe and death.

The vicious woman sometimes reforms if there be dormant virtues which a tactful master can arouse. She will not voluntarily go to a home for fallen women, but when in distress she will steal, go to prison, and thereafter follow a criminal career. She will become the companion of a thief, faithful to him while he treats her well, dropping him if he ill treats her or goes to prison. Late in life these young sinners become saints if they have the means, sots if they have not.

THE WRETCHES

Those who are instinctively vicious take up a criminal career early, never reform, and generally end their days in prison.

Many of the peripatetic sisterhood are infected with disease as the result of the lives they lead, or receive the germs of such disease as heirlooms. The disease itself does not cause death, but it is a very unfavorable complication in any other disease, and tends to shorten their lives. Many die from criminal operations which they perform upon themselves or permit to be performed upon them by their companions or by some physician who makes a specialty of such work.

Most of them wear wedding rings, some acquired in the orthodox way, with a certificate to prove it, others buying the rings for a few cents at a second-hand jewelry store.

The women, however, rarely marry after having taken up their trade on the street. Cases are known where a woman has insisted upon marriage before accompanying a partly-intoxicated man to a hotel. In these cases the men were obliged either to pay heavy blackmail or to use legal measures to get rid of their encumbrance. There are, however, cases where reputable men have married women who had led dissolute lives, knowing their character, with happy results.

One such woman, now highly respected and spending her days in works of charity and practical philanthropy, was once the mistress of a murderer. Another whose early history is as a sealed book in the circles in which she now moves, is the wife and mentor of a famous national character.

One case is well known in Povertyville on account of the standing of the woman's family, the position of the husband, and the publicity given to the attending circumstances. She forgot that a matinee idol was human until it was too late, and her parents, learning of her condition, turned her out of the house. Soon after she was found in "Mrs. Schneider's" house, where, on account of her beauty and well-known history, she became the most popular inmate of the place. A former admirer who frequently visited the place after she was there made arrangements with Mrs. Schneider to take her to a ball, paying the madam the highest charge, for which the girl was permitted to wear the best dress and the most expensive jewelry the establishment possessed. Instead of going to the ball, however, the couple were driven to Jersey City, where he had fitted up a suite of rooms, and they were married. He held a small political office at the time (he has held higher ones since), and his political leader protected him, while madam quietly pocketed her loss. He and his wife have saved many girls, situated as she was once, from becoming wretches on the street.

The wretches of the Tenderloin and other uptown districts have more opportunities to marry than their poorer sisters of the lower east side, as they are, as a rule, more attractive, more refined, better educated, dress better and make greater efforts to gain and retain the affections of an admirer. The female wretches of Povertyville realize that no respectable man would marry one of them, except, perhaps, an old sweetheart who is still infatuated, or a man who would make the sacrifice in order to reform one. Sometimes a partly intoxicated fellow will make an offer of marriage, or a pander will make such an offer so as to live upon the proceeds of her trade. Such offers are naturally rejected. If an offer comes from the man who first ruined her, she will accept without hesitation, as he cannot reproach her later for the life she led, he having made her what she had become. Fallen women invariably retain a kindly affection for the man who caused their downfall. Despising men as a rule, especially those who hire them, they never blame their first lover, but always charge themselves for their weakness.

When women are instinctively bad they will reject all offers, or may accept one for the purpose of blackmail. Such women will not bind themselves through any desire for respectability. When a fallen woman is not instinctively bad, and an offer of marriage is made to her by one who is infatuated with her, she will make the man understand the seriousness of the step he is taking. The fear of future reproach may cause such offer to be rejected. If the man is, however, willing to accept the responsibility she will not say no. The offer of a man who will make so great a sacrifice in order to reform the woman is rejected by the vicious and by the giddy. If made to a woman who has been driven to the street through want or to one who had been a good girl until the time her lover deserted her, such an offer would be accepted, and she will thank providence for the greatest fortune that can fall to a woman of her class. When a man makes a great sacrifice for a woman of this kind by marrying her or receiving her into his household (a dangerous experiment, by the way), she shows true affection for him, accommodates herself to her new position, and becomes the most devout of women and most devoted of wives. Such is not, however, always possible.

A young woman who came from the country, where she had been deserted by her lover when he found that she was in trouble, was in a brothel and on the street for several years. A man connected with a philanthropic organization occasionally visited her, enjoyed her favors, yet preached morality to her. She told him she would gladly give up her calling if someone would marry her. He proposed to her, they were married and settled down in furnished rooms for a week, until he had furnished a flat. There was trouble from the start. She knew nothing of housekeeping, could not prepare a meal, and could not accommodate herself to the change from her former mode of life. The husband, with admirable patience, gave up his house and returned with his wife to the furnished room, taking meals at a restaurant. The birth of a child, and reconciliation with her family, saved this woman from going back to the street.

A similar case did not turn out so well. A mechanic on the east side married a woman of the street, who expressed her desire to become a good, respected wife. Within a few weeks she tired of the monotony of home life, and one evening her husband found a note on the table informing him that his wife felt lonely and went out to see some friends. He found her in a dive, and left her there.

As a rule, when a fallen woman marries she is sincere in her efforts at reformation, and with her past buried she becomes respected and often honored in circles where her old life is unknown.

PART III

THE PROBLEM

THE PROBLEM

CHAPTER I

PHILANTHROPY VS. HYPOCRISY.

CHARITY covers a multitude of sins, but what sins are committed in its name, ask the wretches of Povertyville.

Sins of omission and sins of commission, frauds upon the charitable donors and frauds upon the miserable beneficiaries, hypocrisy under the sign of the cross, and deceit in the name of salvation; all these are found in Povertyville, labeled Charity and Philanthropy.

True, it is but a moiety of the immense amount of charity done in the district; but that little throws a shadow of doubt and discredit far wider than its own area.

The philanthropy which enriches itself at the expense of its beneficiaries, the charity which demands from its recipients more than full value for its charitable gifts, are frauds pure and simple. They are dishonest to giver and receiver alike. In the expressive language of the street,

THE BREAD LINE.

"Someone gets the coin, the others get the laugh." Far worse in its effects upon the recipient is that form of philanthropy which fosters hypocrisy by offering material inducements to those who accept its spiritual gifts.

Of the class selling their gifts, the most barefaced frauds are the free medical institutes on and near the Bowery. These are generally run in connection with drug stores. They have signs in the window announcing "Free Medical Treatment." The applicant is ushered into a small room adjoining or behind the store, where a physician makes a perfunctory examination. Name, address and occupation are entered in a register, and the doctor inquires how he is fixed financially. If the patient can pay nothing for medicine and can leave nothing of value as a deposit for medicine, he is told to go to the hospital. If he can pay for the medicine he receives a prescription written in a ciper, so that it cannot be prepared anywhere but in that drug store. The charge for the medicine is one dollar or more, of which the doctor receives half. Surgical operations are not performed unless the fee is paid in advance, and no one receives a prescription unless he can pay enough for the medicine to include the doctor's commission. These institutes violate the dispensary law, but escape through a technicality.

No objection can be made to philanthropic institutions and organizations which ask for contributions from a charitable public, when they charge their beneficiaries nominal fees and prices. But when an organization posing as a philanthropy charges its beneficiaries the ordinary prices charged by money-making business men for the same commodities or services, it can properly be classed as a "money-making charity." This charge is strengthened when in its appeals for contributions it presents its business venture as a philanthropy.

A well known temperance society, a highly respectable organization, has for its object the promotion of temperance, the reformation of the intemperate, the removal of the causes which lead to intemperance, and the issue of temperance publications. To further these objects, a woman's auxiliary maintains lunch wagons in various parts of the city, and had a restaurant on the Bowery. It is inconceivable how the objects of the society are furthered by establishing lunch wagons and restaurants to compete with other restaurants nearby.

The restaurant furnished meals differing little in quality, quantity or price from meals furnished in other Bowery restaurants, and if it were managed as the others are, it should have been a well-paying enterprise. The lunch wagons furnished over three hundred and seventy thousand meals in one year, the income from this source being over thirty-seven thousand dollars.

It is easy to compute the profits from its restaurant business when it is remembered that the lunch wagons pay no rent, the society claiming they are used for a philanthropic purpose, and the ordinary meal consists of a sandwich and a cup of coffee. Yet this organization asks an indulgent public to contribute towards its support.

There was another restaurant near the one just mentioned which was presented to a charitable public as a philanthropy, but which on the Bowery was supposed to be one of the best-paying establishments on the street. It was maintained by the owner of a sectarian weekly, and in his appeal for funds he mentioned this restaurant in which thousands of men receive "good, substantial" meals for five cents. The meals were worth no more than the price paid for them. It is now run by a private firm.

Of all the pseudo-philanthropies none have the effrontery of an exchange for woman's work, maintained by a number of wealthy women, which charges applicants for positions fifty cents registration fee, charges subscribers two dollars a year for the privilege of admitting one woman's work to its salesrooms, charges ten per cent commission on all sales made there, yet poses as a charity asking for donations to carry on its business venture. As it receives, however, work from "gentlewomen only," the wretches of Povertyville are probably not eligible to its charity.

There are charitable organizations appealing for contributions to carry on work in Povertyville, fully covered by other bodies, and charging for services furnished gratuitously by the state and by other societies.

An employment agency incorporated under a long religious title is one of these. Organized to assist respectable working women to obtain employment, it states in its appeal that no worthy applicant will be denied the aid of the society. It also adds that a fee is charged for every service rendered. The state and many private societies recognize the fact that the gratuitous service of securing work for a person is the least likely to pauperize, and the payment of a registration fee is a hardship to an unemployed person. Other employment agencies run in the name of benevolent societies charge for registration and other services, but they do not ask the public to support this branch of their work.

The Salvation Army is not free from the charge that mercenary motives are back of some of its enterprises. Its old workingman's hotel on the Bowery does not differ from the other lodging houses of the same class, and pays, or ought to pay, as well as the others. The new workingman's hotel, at Chatham Square, is brighter, cleaner, and has more conveniences than the ordinary cheap lodging house. Still, on account of the large number of rooms, it is probably the best-paying lodging house in the city.

The Bowery branch of the Y. M. C. A. is not, and is not intended to be, a money-making philanthropy. It charges fifteen cents for a bed and five cents for a meal, but the majority of the applicants receive free lodging and many receive free meals.

THE PROBLEM

There are many charities in Povertyville which have no money-making features, yet benefit the wretches as little as those we have mentioned. One organization, having an annual income of fifteen hundred dollars, spends one thousand dollars for salaries, rent, and stationery. The rest goes for charity. Another benevolent society, which gives balls and entertainments, "the proceeds going to charity," has a sewing class, and beside receiving dues, contributions and donations, collects over five thousand dollars a year. Yet, after deducting expenses, less than three hundred dollars are left for the relief of the destitute.

Among the hypocritical philanthropists are some of the missions and some organizations making a great display by public distribution of their charitable gifts.

One of the latter class makes several distributions annually, the recipients standing in line to receive their dole, the members and donors standing about watching the proceedings as they would the antics of a freak in a museum. The proverb, "Let not thy right hand know," etc., is out of place at these exhibitions, for the donors apparently look for gratitude from the poor wretches, and seem to derive pleasure in their humiliation. Certainly nothing can crush the spirit more effectually than to make public acknowledgment that one is a pauper.

The master throws the dog a bone and kicks him when he picks it up. This is one form of Christian Charity.

Equally repellant to the sensitive nature is the distribution of Thanksgiving and Christmas dinners in public. While such distributions serve the practical purpose of furnishing a good meal to the needy, and the ulterior purpose of rousing the sympathies of the benevolent by bringing them face to face with those in want, they also benefit many shiftless, worthless fellows, but tend to increase pauperism by leading many self-respecting poor to accept alms and charity.

On Christmas day, 1904, twelve thousand men were needed to clean the streets at two dollars a day. Less than four thousand applied for work, yet forty thousand received free public Christmas dinners from various organizations.

The missions which offer free meals and lodgings as an inducement to the wretches to attend services foster thereby hypocrisy. In 1908 the joint application bureau of the Charity Organization Society and the Association for Improving the Condition of the Poor issued 5,300 personal invitations to men in the bread lines to apply at the bureau for work. Only 136 applied, and most of these refused work. No more emphatic proof need be given to show the general worthlessness of these men. Yet the Bowery Mission maintains its bread line and asks for contributions for its support.

In winter the missions are comfortably filled every night by poor devils who seek shelter from the cold, by homeless men who receive free lodgings through the missions, by many who find pastime in listening to the testimony of the rounders and joining in the singing, and by some who come for spiritual consolation.

On food distribution nights early arrivals are almost without exception tramps and others who come for a free meal. On such nights the mission hall is crowded to the doors. On hot summer nights the services are poorly attended except on distribution nights. Lately (January, 1909) one mission gave breakfasts, evening lunches and maintains a bread line.

Those who understand the character of these wretched beings, outcasts, paupers, the vicious and depraved, pity the credulous, well-intentioned men and women who spend time and money in the wrong direction to regenerate these hopeless cases. They seem to place implicit faith in the "horrible examples" who mount the little mission stage and in apparent meekness give their testimony. These tell hearers that they had led a life of shame, of vice, of depravity, but the Lord found them in the gutter and lifted them up and now they will follow in His steps, etc. For free meals and lodgings most of them will pose as the horrible example or the reformed drunkard, although they cannot maintain the latter pose long.

Occasionally song and prayer will recall tender memories and rouse a dormant conscience, but unless these are sustained by something more substantial, neither memory nor conscience will supply the bed, nor satisfy the craving for the night-cap.

In rare cases there is a true revival of religious feeling, or even a creation of religious feeling in one who has never had that sentiment. They leave the services fully determined to lead good, virtuous lives. But environment and necessity break the firmest resolutions. Religion may give the strength to withstand the jeers of companions, it may renew hope in the future and rouse ambition, but it will not give the physical power to withstand the pangs of hunger nor can it be used as a material cloak to keep off the cold.

From men they become wretches again and follow in the footsteps of the rounders who make the tour of the missions, professing conversion whenever such profession promises to be followed by material benefits.

There are, indeed, some who through the missions have been restored to respectability, some who had resolved to lead better lives and had found an opportunity to do so before necessity drove them back, some who were kept from wandering from the right path. But altogether the actual good done by the missions is outweighed by the harm they do in unconsciously fostering hypocrisy and deceit, and in aiding worthless wretches.

The good intentions of the mission workers, are, however, acknowledged by the wretches and there is no one

THE PROBLEM 257

to whom more deference is shown by them than to Mrs. Bird, the good mother of the Bowery Mission.

One feature of the work of the Salvation Army which savors of hypocrisy, or worse, is the sale of the "War Cry," its official organ, in dives, concert halls and saloons. The women of the Salvation Army enter these places, not to do Evangelical work by the distribution of War Crys as tracts, but they come as newspaper vendors to sell their wares. Their religious garb saves them from abuse. They are engaged in a purely business enterprise, as much a business as the sale of any other publication would be, their mission is mercenary, and the cloak and cap of religion cannot save them from the charge that they are carrying on a regular business by very reprehensible methods.

These are but a few of the many instances in which the charitable givers are imposed upon and the unfortunate receivers derive little benefit from their beneficiaries.

Some of these mentioned are not intended for the classes with which we are dealing, but all are open to the same charge. The good is dissipated in its transmission and the poor devil receives but a shadow and a smell of the donor's gift.

It may seem presumptuous to impugn the motives of men and organizations which have gained worldwide reputations for their philanthropic work. Unquestionably they do some good and are therefore permitted to continue in their work. But motives may always be questioned when we find men becoming wealthy through their connection with philanthropies, when they apply for contributions for business ventures, when almost the entire amount obtained by a philanthropic organization from contributions is used to pay big salaries to officials. It is not within the province of this book to analyze the reports of philanthropies working in Povertyville. Some give detailed accounts which are easily verified; when they give general figures which defy analysis and especially when run by a single individual or a small board, it is impossible to say how much, if any, is "graft."

Methods and measures may in like manner be questioned when they result in perpetuating vice and pauperism by supporting the vicious, shiftless and lazy, instead of making them self-supporting.

CHAPTER II

IMPRACTICABLE IDEALS.

WHEN the idealists and moral philosophers discover a means to eliminate from human nature those passions which beget crime and vice, they will be able to eradicate crime and vice themselves. Until they can accomplish this, their efforts must be limited to the control and repression of those passions.

Under the social and economic conditions of the present time when there is no standard of virtue save such as conscience sets up, and no judgment of vice save such as public policy decrees, when the conception of right and wrong differs with every individual and public policy is forever changing, idealists themselves grope in the dark to find a plane acceptable to all.

Virtue and vice are but relative terms, even crime itself being, under some circumstances, in line with public policy, hence a conditional virtue. We have justifiable homicide, the justification being based upon a legal assumption, as in the killing of a burglar, yet the underlying motive is revenge, as in deliberate and premeditated murder.

The church raffle is a virtue because it wears the cloak of religion, yet it is the outcome of the same vicious gambling instinct which makes the unlawful turkey raffle attractive.

The dealer in futures on the stock market is a legalized speculator, while the dealer in futures in the pool room is a criminal. One speculates upon the outcome of deals which may be influenced by an act of Providence, but are more often influenced by financial trickery, while the bookmaker speculates upon the outcome of a perhaps honestly conducted horse race.

The stock broker whose skillfully worded circulars induce thousands to invest money in worthless stocks, is a respected financier, while the green goods man whose skillfully worded circulars tempt the honest farmers to buy worthless paper goes to prison. So, too, the three card monte man is a criminal, although the victim has one-third of the chances in his favor.

Lottery, forbidden in the United States, was once sanctioned here and is to-day conducted by several foreign governments. Thus we see that public policy is the deciding factor in the estimation of many forms of vice. Even such vices as are not based upon the animal passions are vices or virtues, are justifiable, excusable, or intolerable as public policy may from time to time decide.

Equivocal divorce laws make it possible to commit bigamy legally, a man may have a mistress and a wife,

THE PROBLEM

and the female voluptuary may dispense her favors to a lover or two without losing prestige or violating a statute.

The chorus girl is sought by admirers who pay liberally for her favors; one may even marry her out of selfishness, and she loses neither caste nor respect. Let her lose her charms so that she is compelled to look for admirers and patrons and she becomes a criminal. It is all in the point of view, in the position the person holds, in the individual conception of right and wrong.

It is far from our purpose to extenuate crime and vice. But to show the utter futility of fixing a rational standard of virtue applicable to all places and times, and the folly of endeavoring to eradicate vices and crimes which spring from natural human passions, it is necessary to view both sides of the question and in all its lights. It is necessary to recognize those evils which depend upon the natural appetite and which no human law can suppress, those evils arising out of economic conditions, and those evils which public policy or party politics now class as crimes and again as lawful pastimes or pursuits.

The idealist apparently does not differentiate between these three distinct classes, but would wipe out every act, pursuit and pastime which does not meet with his approval. He sets up his own ideas as the standard of virtue and poses as the immaculate specimen of what the world should be. His ideal city is peopled with beings like himself. There is no vice, no crime, no poverty, no saloon, no dive, no Raines Law hotel, no gambling house. Neither has it a thief, a confidence man, a speculator, a woman walking the street, a beggar nor a tramp. Carrying his conception further, there would be no police, no repressive laws—in short, his ideal city would be a Utopia, such as Moore and Bellamy dreamt of.

Alas, our idealist leaves out of his reckoning human nature. He does not consider the gambling or speculative instinct which underlies the option on next winter's wheat as well as picking the winner in next year's Suburban, the drawing of the church raffle as well as the fall of the die.

He does not consider that sense which begets lust, in his warfare against fallen women. He forgets that that instinct is irrepressible and those who seek these women will find them, or more grossly violate nature's laws. He does not consider economic conditions which produce hard times when persons are driven to crime in self-preservation. He does not stop to think that party politics may cause the enactment of laws which public opinion opposes and the masses will violate without conscientious scruples, making themselves virtual law-breakers. He does not know that some forms of vice are due to mental perversions, are symptoms of disease requiring medical treatment and not repressive punishment.

Each of these factors must be considered in its relations to the individual and to the body politic before rational conclusions can be drawn and measures adopted

THE PROBLEM

to limit vice and crime and prevent their spread. Natural human instincts must always be reckoned with. When some years ago the attempt was made to suppress brothels and drive the women off the street, the wretches sought shelter in the tenements. Hundreds of working girls were thrown in direct contact with the wretches, saw with what ease the latter made a living without work, and followed their example. In one tenement house in East 13th Street in which "Mrs. Gray" found shelter after she had been driven from a brothel, four respectable girls were initiated by Mrs. Gray into the secrets of her vocation and two wives were taught how to earn illicit pin money without danger. In the tenements husbands and sons who had never visited a brothel became the patrons of the wretches, while many of the former patrons were driven to other measures, some even to force, to satisfy their desires.

The eradication of the social evil, and the suppression of the sale of liquor, seem to be the special hobbies of the reformers. Notwithstanding all that has been said and shown to prove that the social evil is a necessary evil in a city having a large floating population, especially in a seaport, reformers still insist upon its total suppression. Whenever they have been given the power to carry out their plans in this direction, their worse than futile efforts have spread the evil, giving it undue publicity, and increased other forms of vice.

Equally unsuccessful have been the efforts made to restrict and suppress drunkenness through suppression of the liquor traffic. Instead of working upon individual cases of drunkenness, they attempt to restrict or suppress the sale of liquor, forgetting that the number of saloons bears no relation to drunkenness or to the amount of liquor consumed.

New York City, with 10,821 saloons, had 71,573 arrests for drunkenness in 1902, an average of 6.6 per saloon. At the same time Philadelphia had an average of 17.5 and Boston 19.8. Cincinnati and San Francisco have about the same population, yet the former, with 1,676 saloons, had less than 2,000 arrests for drunkenness in 1902, while the latter, with 3,052 saloons, had nearly 15,000 arrests in the same time. Toledo, with a population of 150,000 and 660 saloons, had but 343 arrests for drunkenness.

That neither high license nor total prohibition had any bearing upon drunkenness can be seen by other comparisons.

The city of Lawrence, with a license fee of $2,500 and 62 saloons, had 1,321 arrests, one out of every 50 of its population, while Evansville, with a license fee of $75 and 292 saloons, had 345 arrests, or one out of every 219 of its population. Philadelphia, a high license city with twice the population of St. Louis and about half as many saloons, had seven and a half times as many drunks. Cambridge, a temperance town without a saloon, and

92,000 population, had 1,620 drunks, or as many as Newark with a population of a quarter of a million and 1,280 saloons.

Portland, Maine, another temperance town, had more drunks than Indianapolis, which has more than three times the population and 525 saloons.

While a high license fee reduces the number of saloons, even the total suppression of the saloons will not restrict drinking and drunkenness. Notwithstanding the evident conclusions which one must draw from the comparative statistics, reformers still try to force their pet hobbies, making a political issue out of the liquor question. In New York State the liquor question has ceased to be one of morals, but has been converted into a political weapon by the great political parties.

With the exception of the war upon policy playing by the anti-policy society the reformers make no concentrated efforts to curb the gambling and speculative instincts. They leave the vices and crimes dependent thereon to be handled by the police according to the temper of that mercurial body.

Neither do the reformers touch such crimes as theft, fraud, etc.—crimes dependent upon economic conditions—nor would they handle the drug vices, all of which are more amenable to treatment than their own hobbies.

Not alone individuals but organizations, some numbering thousands of members, attempt to bring about impracticable ideals.

A national organization, which in its old name declared its purpose to be the Prevention of State Regulation of Vice, is one of these. Beside the object indicated in its former name, it endeavors to "repress vice, protect the young, rescue the fallen, extend the White Cross among men and maintain the law of purity as binding upon men and women alike." It issues a quarterly magazine and a number of leaflets. Its members are naturally in sympathy with its objects and these are reached by its publications, but aside from the mischievous meddling in a small way politically, when the question of the regulation of vice is brought up, it has no effect upon the class for whose good it claims to labor.

Another National Organization for the Promotion of Social Purity has a more extended scope than the other, and works on more rational lines. Instead of distributing publications among its supporters it works directly upon those it would benefit by the formation of clubs, furnishing girls with employment and prosecuting men who deceive them.

The American Sabbath Union is another body endeavoring to carry out an impracticable ideal, although its work does not bear directly upon our subject. Its object is to preserve the Sabbath as a day of rest and worship, and in its efforts to carry out its object it has tried to enforce measures opposed to public policy, measures to prevent necessary labor on the Sabbath, measures to deprive the great mass of people who work throughout the week of recreation.

The liberal views held by the city magistrates and the common-sense decisions rendered by them on this subject have nullified the misdirected efforts of this body.

It is the natural result which follows any attempt to enforce "Blue Laws" or cram religion down the throat of a complex community.

The New York Sabbath Committee, a local organization, works on similar lines. It is more aggressive than the other, but recognizes local conditions and has more liberal views.

Temperance organizations generally work along similar lines. They carry out their object to prevent drunkenness by enlisting the young, impressing them with the advantages of sobriety and the dangers of drink. The Woman's Christian Temperance Union starts out with the impracticable idea that the way to prevent drunkenness is to forbid the liquor traffic entirely.

When, in 1854, the legislature of the State of New York passed a prohibition law the governor vetoed it, and when a similar bill, passed in 1855, was signed by the governor, the mayor of the City of New York refused to carry out its provisions on the ground that it infringed upon personal liberty and was opposed to the sentiment of the vast majority of the residents of this city. It was declared unconstitutional in 1856. The present high-license law has been especially unfortunate for New York City, although it has added large sums to the city and state treasuries. It has wiped out hundreds of small beer saloons and these were replaced by liquor stores. In the beer saloons men would sit at the tables, spending half an hour or more over a single glass. Now they stand at the bar and will take several glasses where they formerly took one or two. The first noticeable effect of the law was an increase of drinking in the house and family, boxes of bottled beer taking the place of the occasional pint.

It is not within the scope of this work to consider the numerous impracticable measures brought forward to relieve poverty and repress chronic pauperism.

In dealing with the floaters of Povertyville, with a view of uplifting them or ridding the city of them, such extreme measures have been advocated as forcible communism, and hastening by force the natural result of over-population.

Of the more rational measures to improve morally the classes with which we deal may be mentioned the work of the Salvation Army, the Volunteers of America and the Missions.

As a religious movement the success of the Salvation Army and the Volunteers of America is unquestioned. Both have done valuable evangelical work in the slums, whereby they have gained recruits who would otherwise have gone down to the depths of infamy. Whatever may be thought of their methods, they have succeeded in uplifting individuals, making good men and women out of wretches. We may scoff at their bass drum and cymbal processions, we may charge them with hypocrisy in maintaining as philanthropic enterprises well-paying lodging houses, we may denounce the sending of women into disreputable houses to sell War Crys, we may criticise their public distribution of meals, tending, as it certainly does, to foster pauperism and dull the sense of independence in the self-respecting poor, we may even question their honesty of purpose; yet the one great fact remains that they do good. By personal effort in individual cases they drag from the whirlpool, here a drunkard, there a fallen woman, and again the ex-convict drifting back into his old life.

To what extent the mission services tend to reclaim the wretches is problematic. Without some more substantial support than prayer it is doubtful if a single individual among the wretches could be led to a righteous, self-supporting life.

The idealist who thinks that moral teachings alone will suffice to reform the fallen and the depraved cannot realize that there are minds impervious to ideas of morality, that neither prayers nor sermons will fill an empty stomach nor will they destroy the desire for drink. Missions may aid in re-establishing self-respect and manhood; but it requires a material impetus to start the change in the moral character. After a hearty meal we can listen complaisantly to a sermon and imbibe its import, but let the listener suffer the pangs of hunger or the horrible gnawing which accompanies the deprivation of the accustomed drug, or worry about his "hote money," and the most impressive lesson will fall upon inattentive ears.

Neither will mission services rouse the dulled conscience of the depraved even if it were possible to induce these people to attend such services. There is lacking that personal, concentrated interest and attention which is necessary to touch the heart and reason of the hardened wretch. Herein lies the secret of the success of the workers who take individual cases and by heart-to-heart talks, behind closed doors, arouse a sense of honor and laudable ambition in the breast of the listener.

Any work which lessens a vicious phase of city life is commendable. The Committee of Fourteen, which was organized to suppress the vicious Raines Law hotels, has succeeded in securing a modification of the original law whereby the number of such resorts was reduced from over 1,400, in existence when the committee was formed in 1905, to about 860 in May, 1906. Of these not more than 250 are legitimate hotels. Since 1906 their efforts have been directed toward securing the enforcement of the law. The aggressive secretary of the committee has forced the revocation of the licenses of a number of the most notorious of these brothel hotels, in spite of powerful political and financial opposition.

The City Vigilance League has looked after the police end of such resorts, its secretary being responsible for many of the police raids on dives and brothels. While these two organizations have improved the moral aspect of the city by wiping out many dives and Raines Law hotels, they have done nothing to lessen the prevalence of the vice and their work actually benefits the foul resorts, which can carry out the provisions of the vicious Raines Law.

CHAPTER III

PRACTICAL MEASURES.

MAN is a gregarious animal, having, in common with the rest of the animal kingdom, the physical instincts of self-preservation and propagation. He has, besides, the human, mental instincts, a self-directing will and reason to follow his physical instincts, and a spiritual mentor, conscience, to direct will and reason to move in proper channels.

Knowing the nature of pain, one of the ends to be attained by civilization is a happiness which gives no pain, mental or physical, in its acquisition or possession; hence force is to be used only as a last resort in the pursuit of happiness.

Reason, will and conscience, inherent in the human being as a germ, must be developed, and the form of development depends upon education and environment. Yet not alone individuals but neighboring communities having the same advantages of education and environment differ vastly in their ideals, in the dictates of conscience, even in the reasoning faculties. Although they may be on the same plane of civilization they try to attain the same end—the acquistion of happiness—by following a different course from that of their neighbors. Reason invents substitutes for the force employed by the savage in following his physical instincts, and each one employs the substitute which he supposes will lead to the end in view most speedily, with the least labor and the least inconvenience or pain to others. It is when that substitute does annoy or pain the neighbor that measures must be taken to interfere with the offender's actions. This applies as well to nations and communities as to the individuals with whom we are dealing. Public policy decrees that not only must the body as a whole interfere when one man's actions injure another, such action constituting a crime, but when a man's action be of such a nature that he is himself injured thereby. When his morals are involved it is a vice. It is then the duty, not alone of the individual injured, but of the whole community, to suppress vice and crime, gently if possible, forcibly if need be. The offender must be led in the right path, and if he will not remain there he must be placed under restraint. But instead of considering the offense only and applying measures based upon the gravity of the crime, the offender's mental and moral condition should be first considered. Is his lapse due to depravity or a perverted conscience and reason, or is it due to ignorance or a not fully developed conscience and reason, or is it due to necessity which may temporarily dull the spiritual instinct? Each cause demands a distinctive method of treatment. Local conditions may make a restriction of rational, normal acts necessary, declaring such to be crimes, although no moral law is violated. The fault may even be a recognized disease which it would be criminal to call a crime.

Once they hung the thief, burnt the witch, branded the dissolute woman and sold the pauper. Then heavy drinking was an accomplishment, as was blasphemy, while the honor of womanhood was a bauble, priceless as a new toy to the maid, valueless as an old toy later.

Now motive and mind are considered as well as the crime itself. The old legal adage, "Let the punishment fit the crime," has lost its force. We consider (or should do so) when we punish, how far it may reform the offender, how it may be an example to others and how society may be safeguarded from a repetition of the act.

These are the underlying principles of punishment. It also involves another principle or sentiment, revenge, expressed by one writer as "the indignation of society which has been outraged by the violation of its laws."

But the form of punishment universally adopted at present, namely, imprisonment, only stimulates the fear of physical discomfiture and possible pain, without improving either the mind or conscience. As a deterrent influence it is often successful, as a reforming influence it is an absolute failure. It is of service to society only in cases which withstand efforts to correct moral perversion and then it is a safeguard, but neither an example nor a lesson. Crime and vice due to ignorance are best treated by educational measures, religious and social, while neither education nor imprisonment will avail where necessity dulls conscience.

In cases in which there is a physical or mental defect, those moral perversions properly classed as manias, medical treatment is indicated. It is extremely difficult, however, to fix the dividing line between kleptomania, or the mania for stealing, and criminal theft. Many thieves steal because they cannot resist the temptation when placed before them. The kleptomaniac presents the same plea. The social standing of the offender and the character of the booty are usually the deciding factors when the question of kleptomania is raised. A wealthy woman pockets trinkets of little value at the bargain counter and is caught. Her plea of "kleptomania" is accepted. A poor girl caught in the same act is a shoplifter, although the theft may have been committed under the same moral perversion or uncontrollable impulse.

When a supposedly wealthy woman steals a four thousand dollar diamond necklace she presents a plea of temporary aberration of mind, and there is none to disprove it. She passes as a kleptomaniac.

The husband of a prominent actress, a man of some means and very charitable, is a true kleptomaniac, and is known for this failing in the establishments in which he deals. While making expensive purchases he will pocket articles of little value. He has been known to carry off a weight from the scales, a child's shoe, a newspaper, and other small articles, paying for them if detected. Where his failing is known, he is carefully watched, every article he takes is noted, and a bill is sent to him the same day. Such bills are invariably paid without question. This is true kleptomania, and no punitive measures will cure the disease. Fear of exposure when caught has a deterrent effect, but medical treatment and the knowledge that one is constantly watched may effect a cure.

A factor which can be overlooked in small towns, but not in large cities, is the social evil. It has been shown that this is a necessary evil wherever there is a large floating population, and some foreign governments, recognizing the necessity for such women, have passed laws regulating their vocation. If we consider their calling criminal, we must consider man's animal passions, which necessitates this calling, as moral perversions, criminal or diseased. Yet these passions are due to the procreative instinct common throughout the animal kingdom.

There is no uniformity in the state laws passed to restrict this vocation, nor in their enforcement. Nor is there any uniformity in the interpretation of these laws by judges, some enforcing them with the utmost rigor, others, recognizing the necessity of this evil, refusing to enforce them at all. On the night of August 13th, 1903, thirty-two women were arrested for soliciting on the streets of New York City. All were discharged by the police justice the following morning. Since the institution of the night courts in New York such women are brought before this court. Those arrested for soliciting are either fined, imprisoned or placed in charge of a probation officer, while those caught in raided dives are usually discharged.

Another factor which must be considered when taking up measures for the suppression of vice and crime is the passion for gambling and speculating. There is no dividing line between the two—the latter is permitted by law, the former forbidden. Public policy, and not conscience or reason, decides where one begins and the other ends.

As for the general alleviation of poverty and the eradication of pauperism, these belong properly to the realm of the social economists. Measures can, however, be taken to relieve the particular class with whom we are dealing, but here, too, measures must be based upon individual cases. The cause in each case must be considered, the person's wants and needs, his intelligence and adaptability, his willingness and ability, all must be taken into account. This is the plan followed by the Charity Organization Society.

Where these factors are disregarded and all are considered as part of a whole, with measures applied to all alike, all are forced into the same plane, that of the pauper.

At the great Salvation Army dinners we see tramps, worthless, shiftless, able-bodied men, enjoying the bounty of the charitable, and alongside of them are little children, unconscious of their position, mothers submitting to the humiliation of appearing in public as paupers in order to obtain a good meal for themselves and little ones, and men, self-respecting up to the moment when first driven to break the bitter bread of charity with tramps and beggars under the public gaze, as paupers.

We will endeavor to show how individual efforts, properly directed, with due regard for the mental, moral and physical capacity of the person, may lead to the reformation and betterment of the wretches.

The first step should be the elimination of pseudo-charities and those fostering pauperism.

The warden of a city prison declared that while some of his "guests" never return after their first visit, those who come a second time invariably come again.

The habitual criminal never reforms. He may profess reformation, may even lead a proper life for a time, but given the opportunity he will not resist the temptation. (While writing this, a woman, aged 69, was sent to prison for the thirteenth time for shoplifting, ten years having elapsed since her last offense.)

The safety of society demands that such persons be kept under constant restraint or watch, and the power now given to magistrates to make the term of imprisonment indefinite, secures the greatest measure of safety compatible with justice and humanity. With many the fear of imprisonment has a less deterrent effect than the fear of physical pain. Some places have established corporal punishment, notably Delaware, for wife beaters. It is a brutal, yet most effective measure, and no one who has been thus punished has repeated the offense.

When one naturally vicious is thrown in contact with criminals he becomes a criminal himself. Imprisonment with the association of habitual offenders, is a hardening process, during which criminal instincts are developed and the young offender comes out worse than before.

Solitary confinement, even for a short time, is a very severe form of punishment, and if inflicted upon the first offense it will keep the offender from contact with hardened criminals.

The deterrent effect of this form of punishment is far greater than a much longer period in the prison workshops, surrounded by fellow convicts. If the offender upon his release from solitary confinement is at once removed from his former surroundings, and placed in such a position that he can have the association of good men and women, with the opportunity to earn a livelihood, such person will lead a righteous life so long as temptation is not placed in his way. He will in time understand that there is a material benefit in being honest and honorable, and will resist temptation, if not from the dictates of conscience, certainly from the dictates of policy and self-interest.

The same line of treatment will avail where the offense arises from ignorance. Instead of solitary confinement, however, educational measures will be more successful. Here religious teaching may rouse a dormant conscience, but the removal of temptation and the stimulation of work among respectable men are necessary to complete the work of reformation. This is the policy followed by the Prison Association. It secures work for the discharged prisoner in places where he is free from temptation, where he comes in contact with good men, where his past is unknown, and he has an opportunity to rehabilitate himself.

There is one fundamental fault with our reformatory and punitive systems.

With the exception of the death penalty for murder there is but one method of punishment, imprisonment, differing only in length of time, for all offenses. There is, indeed, another, the imposition of a fine, an unjust provision which gives the rich a decided advantage over the poor.

Imprisonment may be the proper punishment for the habitual criminal, but many offenses are punished by imprisonment which require entirely different treatment.

A hod carrier, climbing up a ladder, drops a brick from his hod upon the head of a passer-by. He goes to prison for manslaughter. He may be a God-fearing, law-abiding man; he may have been unconscious of the accident until the moment of arrest, yet he must suffer the same punishment meted out to the thief or burglar who is prepared to commit murder when caught in a lesser crime. If the brick had fallen an inch from the passerby, the hod carrier would have been innocent of crime. Had the brick fallen on the victim's shoulder it would have been assault or criminal negligence, but falling on the skull, crushing it, the crime is homicide. His freedom or his length of punishment depends upon the spot where the brick fell. And the punishment for what would be called an act of Providence differs in no wise from the punishment received by the conscienceless wretch who robs a child of its cloak for the price of a drink.

While corporal punishment or a long period of imprisonment will deter the hardened criminal, and solitary confinement will deter the young offender, none of these will have any effect upon the hod carrier.

The pangs of conscience will punish him more than prison.

The poor devil forced to crime through want requires other treatment than the ordinary criminal. Imprisonment and the association of criminals will only embitter him against society and squash whatever conscience remains in him, and he will come out a criminal and follow a criminal career.

Work at living wages will save him, though such work be under government control. Let it be a state farm or workshop, or road-making, or any similar occupation, where he will receive pay for work done, and paying out of his wages for his board. Forcible detention until he has saved a certain amount, the amount determined by the gravity of the crime, would be a fitting penalty for his offense, and would place him in such a position that he would not be immediately forced into crime upon his release.

Hard work, with intervals of solitary confinement, is the only effective method of dealing with that class who live from the earnings of dissolute women.

Unfortunately, there is no law, except that covering vagrancy, by which these fellows can be reached unless they add theft to their vile occupation. The law takes cognizance of the inciter to crime, but the inciter to vice goes free, although his work is more dangerous to society than that of the fagin or fence.

(The term Fagin, after Dickens' notorious character in Oliver Twist, is now generally applied to one who induces children to become pickpockets and shoplifters.)

The pander is a human parasite, without a redeeming virtue, yet his calling as paid protector of lewd women is legitimate, as there is no law covering it.

This fellow is on a lower plane, morally, than the habitual criminal, and only the fear of harsh prison treatment will make him take up honest work and deter him from forcing women to support him. The fence and the fagin cannot be restrained by ordinary prison punishment, while moral teachings are wasted upon these unconscionable wretches. Long periods of imprisonment, with harsh treatment toward the end of their term, would be the most effective method of repressing their vocations.

A week of hard labor has a more deterrent effect upon the tramp than six months of ordinary penitentiary or workhouse labor. The tramp does not mind the abuse, which seems to be a part of the prison routine, but work and wash have a powerful influence for good. Tramps desert localities where they are put to hard work when caught.

One great advantage of the reformatory over the prison is that the inmates learn a trade, by which they can support themselves after their release. This ought to be part of the prison routine, and every prisoner should at his release have some trade.

After a prisoner has worked in a prison quarry for a year or two he is not fit to take up any occupation upon his release, and must go back to crime.

The treatment of women leading vicious or criminal lives is simpler than the treatment of men. Women are, as a rule, impressionable, amenable to religious teachings, and easily deterred by fear of punishment.

Each case, however, requires individual treatment, based upon mental and moral capacity and the consideration of the cause which led her into crime and vice.

Of all the sociological problems none presents greater difficulties than the disposition of the social evil. What shall be done for and with the women whose vocation is embraced in this evil? In small towns where such women are unnecessary, the most stringent measures should be taken to drive them out. In a great city like New York, with a large floating population (estimated here at 60,000), such women are necessary, and acknowledging this necessity, we must recognize the necessity for regulating their vocation. The hypocritical cry "to regulate vice is to legalize vice" is the main obstacle in the way of enacting laws restricting the social evil, and so long as its existence depends upon the temper of the police, no improvement can be expected in the condition of this evil in New York. While there are numerous laws and police regulations touching upon the social evil, the panders and prostitutes and keepers of vicious resorts, some are conflicting, others are impracticable, most are indefinite, thereby allowing magistrates discretionary powers in their interpretation and the police force considerable leeway in their enforcement. Other communities, not suffering from an over-sensitive false modesty, have attacked this problem in a rational manner, restricting the vocation to certain neighborhoods, to certain ages, to women free from disease. They have enacted laws inflicting heavy penalties for violation of the regulations of the social evil. Adding to these enactments summary punishment for men who drive their wives or mistresses to the street to support them, for women who bring their daughters or foundlings up in vice, for men who deceive and then desert their sweethearts, and we restrict the evil to a class of women who will be vile in spite of all that may be done for them.

There may be some driven to this calling through want, but the number will be reduced when they find they must place themselves under police and medical supervision.

The woman driven to the street through want might have been saved before entering upon her career at the expense of a kind word and a few dollars.

After a woman has been driven through want to take up a life of shame, and finds that she can earn more in a night than at another occupation in a week, she will not voluntarily go back to the honest work at which she formerly starved.

In the early part of their careers these women are amenable to religious teachings, backed by material support. Later on, when hardened, they will not reform.

The class recruited from the shops, who receive low wages and must supplement these by giving favors occasionally to friends in gratitude for loans, can be saved from a life of shame by increased wages and friendly supervision.

This involves economic questions beyond the scope of this work. As a business proposition it seems better to expend money in increased wages rather than in charitable donations to homes for fallen women, when women are driven to these homes through insufficient wages.

It is almost impossible to reach that large class of women who dispense favors to employers, superiors or lovers. Most of these, when discarded by their admirers, take up illicit relations with others and when they find that they can earn more this way than by honest work they join the ranks of fallen women. The modern idea in dealing with vicious phases of life is to determine the causes and apply preventive measures, rather than to treat the faults and vices and their results. It is believed that much unchastity can be prevented if young men and women knew the truth about sexual matters, sexual anatomy and physiology and the dangers of unchastity. The American Society of Sanitary and Moral Prophylaxis, in its efforts to limit the spread of diseases arising from the social evil, is endeavoring to spread this knowledge by issuing pamphlets on these subjects. This reaches, however, only one, although a very important one, of the fundamental causes of vice.

The poor girl turned adrift by a false lover, when she is in trouble, can be easily saved at the expense of a little money and some personal effort. Her lover should be compelled to marry her and support her and her offspring. But if he will not, where is the good Samaritan who will take this pitiable wretch into his or her home until her trouble is over, then place her in a position where she can come in contact with good men and women?

THE PROBLEM

Yet men and women have taken pity upon such unfortunates, have shielded them until their day of trial was over, and, leaving the child in a foundling asylum until it could be reclaimed, placed their wards in positions of respectability.

And good men have heard the pitiful confession before they led their wives to the alter and have said as the Master said to the woman which was a sinner, "Thy sins are forgiven; thy faith hath saved thee."

Unfortunately, such girls, when deserted by false lovers, hide their disgrace until their condition betrays them, then they go to a hospital, or a home. Here they are thrown in contact with other women similarly situated and most of them afterwards take up a life of shame.

With the gay and giddy and the naturally vicious, little can be done. The vicious woman may be cowed by fear, but she will not reform. The giddy woman may be influenced by religious teaching while she is young, but she will still seek pleasure and go back to her old life. Occasionally a dormant conscience will be roused and under pleasant conditions a fallen woman may learn that virtue may be materially as well as spiritually profitable. But the lesson must be taught early in her career by a congenial and tactful teacher.

When women of this class are arrested on the usual charge of soliciting they are generally fined or sent to prison for a few days. Neither form of punishment has a deterrent effect.

In the workhouse they are consoled and cheered by older rounders and they come out worse and more determined than ever.

The inconsistency and imperfection of the laws at present in force, bearing upon the social evil, make it impossible to formulate any method of improving this condition under such laws. No one method would avail with all; indeed, with those hardened to the life and without moral instincts, neither force, detention nor teachings would be of any service. Segregation with police supervision would make them harmless to society, but such a course would involve state regulation of vice.

As for the others, the individual efforts of good women who were not ashamed to speak to the wretched beings of the street, have been more successful in reclaiming the wayward and fallen than repressive laws and mission prayers.

The women who follow a criminal course are, as a rule, women hardened by their lives on the street, and those having inherent vices.

They never reform, although in adversity they will seek relief in a reformatory or home. A long term of imprisonment with hard menial labor has a more deterrent effect upon them than upon men. Efforts at reformation are wasted.

NOTE.—This subject is more fully discussed in the author's brochure, "The Social Evil: A Plea."

The old rounders who are drinkers but not criminals are not influenced by imprisonment or work. The most effective method of curing them would be to place them under treatment for the drink habit.

With that class of wretches whose bestial habits have been referred to there is but one rational method of treatment. Their perverted tastes cannot be altered by lectures, prayers or medicines. Solitary confinement and hard labor have a deterrent effect, but a self-imposed companion who would not hesitate to use force whenever the wretch attempts to practice his vice would do more good.

Those suffering from the drug habit are really patients, not criminals, and all but the smokers are anxious to give up the habit. There is no public institution where such cases are treated; private asylums are expensive, and most of the so-called cures are frauds. While there are scores of richly-endowed hospitals in the city there is none which will undertake the treatment of drug habitués. Neither is there an institution which will treat drunkards. The Christian Home for Intemperate Men in Mount Vernon attempts to treat such cases through religious influence, but it has no power to restrain or hold inmates, and such restraint is necessary to effect a permanent cure. The cure of the drug habit is effected by complete deprivation of the drug, treating the dangerous symptoms of collapse as they appear. This requires restraint and the laws of this State forbid such restraint except in the case of insane. An institution conducted by the city or State for the treatment of drug habits and alcoholism would do incalculable good, for many would be restored to health and manhood who are now doomed to go down as sots or fiends.

The opium smoker does not want to be cured and force is often fatal. The vice can, however, be restricted and perhaps, in time, entirely suppressed by regulating the sale of the crude drug, enforcing restrictions now placed upon its sale, forbidding entirely the sale of the prepared "hop," and also of the smoking implements. The more difficult and expensive it becomes to indulge in this vice the fewer will its converts become.

We now come to that great class standing between the honest laboring poor and the vicious and criminal. These are the poor who will not work, the homeless poor in search of work and on the verge of crime, the beggar and the tramp.

Those who want work will not associate with those who will not work. Until the opening of the two Mills hotels the former were thrown in contact with the shiftless and vicious in the lodging houses, with the inevitable result. The latter were not improved, the former were debased. The Mills hotels have segregated the good from the bad, but they cannot hold all who would patronize them. There the law-abiding, self-respecting man comes in contact with others of his own class and similarly situated. When he has reached the end of his resources he must leave the hotel and he is then on the point of becoming a beggar, a thief or a tramp. A few dollars spent upon the poor devil at this time will save him from becoming a wretch and may save the State many times that amount.

Here is a fruitful field yet little touched by the State or by private philanthropy. Is it not better to save a man as he is about to go down, than to drag him up when he is down?

The man who is out of work, without home, friends or resources, reaches a crisis in his life when his last dollar is gone and the pangs of hunger assail him.

Within the next few hours he will have become a suicide, a thief or a street beggar, or else he will apply to some charity for aid.

Some men in desperation will attack a stranger to rob him, yet have not the hardihood to approach a stranger and ask him for the price of a meal. Many when they accept the first meal drop at once in their own estimation from the self-respecting man to the pauper.

Few retain their self-respect and ambition after having been compelled to associate with beggars and tramps.

Those who apply at the Municipal Lodging House know that after three days they are considered vagrants, are sent to the police station, then to the work house.

One might apply to the Charity Organization Society

at 22nd Street and Fourth Avenue. This society will send him to its wood yard, where he will do a few hours' work and receive supper, breakfast and bed.

The work is hard and when one is unaccustomed to hard manual labor it is extremely irksome. This work is, moreover, only temporary.

The Industrial Christian Alliance in Bleecker Street will give him a temporary home. Here more than anywhere else does he feel that he is dependent upon charity, although he is employed at tailoring, carpentering, brushmaking or shoemaking while at the Home. Still it has saved many men who would otherwise have become wretches.

The Salvation Army does similar work, but this, as the other, has religious features which may conflict with the man's conscience. The Bowery branch of the Y. M. C. A. most closely approaches the form of philanthropy required in these cases.

One of the most difficult problems is how to secure work for those who want but cannot find suitable employment.

During periods of industrial depression thousands of men come to this city in search of work. Many possess trades and qualifications for which there is no demand here; others come without references or refer to employers in other cities.

THE PROBLEM 293

Those coming from farming districts have no trade available in the city, while many come from other cities looking for clerical positions.

The latter are soon in trouble, as the supply of clerks far exceeds the demand, and those accustomed to clerical work are unable to stand the strain of prolonged hard labor, and to outdoor exposure.

In February, 1908, thirty out of eighty guests in a Bowery lodging house would tell the writer what their vocations and aims were. Nineteen said they had done clerical work before and fifteen of these had been less than a year in the city.

Most of them were supplied with funds, having made a few dollars shoveling snow during the preceding week. All said they wanted work of any kind, but when closely questioned it was found that not one knew any other trade and could take up nothing but bookkeeping or clerk's work.

Those from out of town said they would go back to where they came from if they could raise the fare.

Some undoubtedly started out on foot when spring set in and are probably still on the tramp. When the police station lodging rooms were closed in the winter of 1898 nearly 1,000 homeless wretches found shelter on a barge furnished by the city. About forty per cent of these were in New York less than two months. When it was announced that those who would not work would be sent to prison as vagrants the daily number dropped from nearly 500 to 120.

It seems to be the most rational and in the end the most economical method of disposing of such cases to send them back to the place from which they came, where they have friends and perhaps relatives who can look after them until they secure employment.

The farmhand is accustomed to outdoor work, is not afraid of hard labor and should have little difficulty in securing employment.

If there were a law compelling contractors to employ none but citizens on public works it would give work to thousands of unemployed Americans who now watch the foreigners imported for the purpose working on public structures. They say the American won't work with pick and shovel, that he foments trouble by inciting others to strike; that even if inclined to do manual labor he cannot or will not accomplish as much as the foreigner, who, in his opinion, does not know half as much as himself; finally, the foreigner will do more for less money than the American.

Some of these charges are undoubtedly true. Many Americans would starve before doing menial work or submit to the dictation of a "boss."

Many, on the other hand, are not ashamed to do any

honest work which will keep them from starvation. These should have an opportunity to work in places now filled by unskilled foreigners.

There are comparatively few skilled laborers among the wretches, and these are almost without exception drunkards.

During a period of business depression, when the number of unemployed men increases, the skilled trades suffer with the others. It is at such times that private philanthropy can do much to prevent the production of paupers.

Private loans of small amounts to those at the turning point will foster self-respect and stimulate energy and ambition, while gifts will have the opposite effect.

At all times a small loan to one who has a trade or profession will produce better results than the same amount given as a charitable gift.

Those who enter Povertyville to sink their identity will oppose every effort to rehabilitate themselves. Family influences may prevail, but neither prayers nor punishment have any effect.

Some of them would even welcome imprisonment, since they can more effectually hide themselves in prison than anywhere else.

The lazy, shiftless fellow who won't work but will beg can be easily suppressed. The same treatment applied to him as has been suggested for the tramp will either convert him into self-supporting citizen or will drive him out of the city.

The harshest measures are necessary to cure the professional beggar. This is the only case where a heavy fine has a more deterrent effect than imprisonment, and if the fine is increased upon each conviction the beggar will seek other fields. The law should be so amended that a few lead pencils in a coat pocket cannot serve as a subterfuge to evade it.

In all cases, except where a fault has been forced upon an offender, as when in dire need, or when a girl has been deceived and deserted, a short, harsh punishment, followed by educational and religious influences, should be tried for a first offense. The removal of temptation, the substitution of innocent pastimes for vicious pleasures, companionship of good men and women, congenial employment where the mind and body both are fully occupied, arousing a sense of personal responsibility, and hiding the dark spot in their past, should be the groundwork on which efforts for reformation should be conducted.

And while such efforts are made to redeem the individual, the state legislature should take cognizance of local conditions and needs and enact laws based upon such conditions and needs. In this respect the city of New York is in an unfortunate position. Although containing about half of the population of the state and paying two-thirds of the state tax, it has but eighty-four out of two hundred and one members in the state legislature. At the present time (1908) fifty-six out of the eighty-four are opposed to the party in power in the state. New York City is consequently at the mercy of rural legislators politically opposed to the city, most of whom are unacquainted with its needs, and who enact laws well suited to a rural population but inapplicable to the metropolis. The city is oppressed by such legislative blunders as the Raines Law, which has scattered disreputable houses all over the city, the excise provisions of which work a hardship upon thousands of citizens, discriminate against the liquor traffic in the city and in favor of this traffic in other places in the state in order to enrich the state treasury; a Sunday law which cannot be enforced, as it is against public policy, and a host of other laws which local magistrates decline to uphold and the police will not enforce. At the present moment we see a police commissioner who is endeavoring to carry out the laws as they are on the statute books at loggerheads with police magistrates who interpret the laws agreeably to the spirit of the times and the needs of the city. The worst possible solution of the problems arising out of these faulty laws is the toleration of their evasion, yet that seems to be the attitude of the community toward them at present. This attitude further strengthens the trend of judicial opinion in questions involving morality and we see, as a result, dives raided by the police and the inmates released by the police magistrates, the keepers of Raines Law hotels arrested on circumstantial evidence, and though there be not the shadow of a doubt that they violate the law, they are discharged for want of absolute proof; a brothel keeper securing an injunction against the police commissioner restraining him from posting an officer in front of the house. There is a growing feeling of indignation in the city against the state and those who try to carry out the state laws literally and rigorously. It is, however, only a question of time when the city's demand for home rule and for laws suitable to its own needs must be heeded by the state legislature.

With the regulation of those evils which are necessary to avoid worse ones, and the strict enforcement of such regulations, with the suppression of those evils which can be suppressed without endangering society or public policy; with the segregation of the virtuous and unfortunate from the vicious and lazy, aiding the former to be self-supporting, repressing the latter by force, if necessary, we may be able to reach a rational ideal in the sociological aspect of our city.

THE END.

NOTE.—This work was written between 1903 and 1906 with some additions and corrections made in the winter of 1908-9. A few of the resorts described have been altered or wiped out and some of the characters have disappeared. The characteristics of the Bowery still remain, although there is a vast improvement in the social conditions in the district. New laws, new tenements, modern schools and public parks have bettered the environment and strengthened home influences among the poor dwellers, but these factors for good do not affect the homeless, vicious, shiftless and criminal classes with whom we are dealing. It is hoped that the completion of the two new bridges which will extend to the Bowery will make this a heavy traffic thoroughfare, that shops, factories and stores will take the place of the resorts of pleasure, vice and poverty, that scientific philanthropy and rational laws will take the place of the useless and pseudo-charities and inconsistent discretionary statutes now dealing with the wretches.

(In Preparation. The Wretches of Upper Tendom)

Filmed by Preservation NEH 1992

Printed in Dunstable, United Kingdom